CAREFREE, LLC
BOOK PUBLISHERS

"Manned flight has done more to change the relations of the earth's inhabitants than any other factor of human endeavor. As an awesome power for good and for evil it has nullified the protection and isolation of traditional frontiers. It has lofted the common man toward hitherto undreamed of destinations, and it has changed forever, the very pattern of his daily existence."

—Ernest K. Gann

# THIS IS YOUR CAPTAIN SPEAKING

RAY STARK

EDITED BY RALPH TANNER

## FLIGHT TRAINING FOR PASSENGERS

*This is Your Captain Speaking*

Cover Design: ATG Productions
Text Illustrations: John Robinson
Book Design/Layout: The Printed Page

ISBN 0-9705621-0-1
Library of Congress Catalog Number: 2002091135

Published by Carefree LLC Book Publishers

First Printing 2002

Manufactured in the United States of America

# Dedication

This book is dedicated to my father and those of his generation. A calm and encouraging instructor, he taught me to fly at an early age. During that time he told me, "If a man can make his hobby his livelihood, by any measure, he may be considered a success. But with that knowledge comes the understanding that once a hobby becomes your livelihood, it is no longer your hobby." This from a man who rode trains during the Great Depression between parents in Oklahoma and California at the age of 12 with his 9-year-old brother in tow. Dad never finished high school but yet taught himself electronics. He was a consummate professional from another era, the likes of which we may never see again.

I carry a little of him with me every time I take to the skies.

Thanks Dad.

# This is Your Captain Speaking

# An Editorial

After September 11, 2001

I first experienced the tragedy of September 11th after landing at Houston Hobby airport in Houston, Texas. The tower controller advised pilots on the tower frequency that, "Two 737's just crashed into the World Trade center. This appears to have been a terrorist act."— The early reports misidentified the aircraft involved. Minutes later, after parking at the gate, I found a small group of people in a closed bar, crowded around a fuzzy TV which framed surreal pictures of the burning twin towers. As I watched replays of the crashes in disbelief, I shared the profound sense of loss for those on the aircraft as well as those on the ground. To me the horror seemed unreal, until I turned around and saw the emotion, not of fear but of anger, on the faces of the travelers who had just flown in on my plane and were now watching in disbelief along with me. We could have been among those who died.

My heart goes out to those who lost loved ones as a result of this heinous act. We have all been touched by this event in one way or another. I have resolved not to surrender to terror, but rather to rise from these reckless acts stronger and more secure about this country. Today, what I see as I travel across America tells me America agrees.

I began writing this book in August of 1999, fully two years before the attack. My manuscript was focused on operational aspects of commercial aviation in an attempt to educate the public as to what happens behind the scenes in commercial aviation, and hopefully in doing so, alleviate some worries. This book was never intended as a treatise on terrorism. Hijackings have been a part of private and commercial aviation for more than 40 years. Every year, millions of planes take off and land across this country. I will not let four incidents perpetrated by criminals stop me from living the unique freedom my country holds so sacred. I will continue to live, albeit more vigilant, but, make no mistake: *I will continue with my life. I will not give in to terrorists.* To do otherwise would be to grant victory to the criminals in this world who do not value human life or the precious freedom we enjoy in this society. I must continue to pursue life's interests for myself, my family, my country, and most importantly, for those whose lives ended needlessly on September 11, 2001.

Captain Ray Stark

# Preface

## Knowledge Over Fear

**For** an estimated 7 million people in the U. S., fear of flying is the biggest impediment to enjoying the fastest and safest mode of transportation yet devised, even before the marginal meals, occasional surly airline personnel, and flight delays. Dealing with fear or uncertainty is often just a matter of learning how things work behind the scenes. When it comes to commercial aviation, those in the know often appear as though they want to keep you in the dark.

This book is intended to answer questions, in varying detail, about what actually happens to you as you travel in the commercial air system. You will begin to understand why things happen as they do, or sometimes do not.

A reasonable amount of worry or concern is understandable when faced with flying. I recently flew to Hawaii on vacation with my family on another airline. In spite of all my experience and training, I had a few moments where I found myself hoping they did things like we do at our airline. Seated in the cabin as a passenger, I was out of control, one of the hundreds in the back of the plane. I thought of the worries passing through the minds of passengers seated on my flights.

As a five-year-old child, flying with my father in our Cessna, I remember sitting on his lap and steering the plane with the yoke, unable to reach the pedals. At that age I knew no fear and trusted him completely. But as I got older and began to think for myself, I began to have reservations about the relative safety of this hobby. One early worry I remember having was, "Hey, what if the wings come off?"

A little knowledge is dangerous. I understood the fundamentals of engineering and began to question the stresses that the wings experience in flight. My father said, "They are really mounted quite solidly. How many instances have you heard of where the wings have fallen off?" His question to my concern grounded me in reality, and I realized that if this were really a problem, planes would be falling out of the sky on a daily basis. I had never heard of this happening and after the realization sunk in, that fear was conquered.

That is, at least until last month. My 18-year-old daughter received her pilot's license and wanted to take her old dad up as her first passenger. My first flight in a Cessna 152 in nearly 30 years brought back many of my initial concerns. I am an Airline Transport Pilot with nearly 16,000 flying hours and that little plane accelerated my heartbeat for the first few minutes until I got used to the way it handled. Watching my daughter calmly and proficiently operate the aircraft, I soon relaxed and realized experience, knowledge, and repetition are essential to truly conquer fear.

Being an airline pilot requires that I occasionally ride in the back of the aircraft, often in uniform. Frequently I have had passengers express to me their trepidation about getting on a plane. In almost every case, with mild humor and my running explanation of what was happening during the flight, I helped the nervous passenger come out of their cocoon of fear and, if but for a moment, see the process for the wonder that it is. In doing so, the person was able to look out the window and actually relax for a few minutes. That has always been rewarding to me: The looks on the faces of these fellow passengers, as we parted, meant I had helped them in some small way conquer, through understanding, a natural fear of the unknown. That is the aim of this book.

This book, for uneasy flyers and experienced flyers alike, will attempt to give the reader a "peek behind the curtain" and give some insight as to why things happen as they do. Some of the topics get technical, and I will do my best to explain these areas. For those I think might be interested, I wander off into some subjects a little deeper, but if that doesn't interest you, skip over these italicized paragraphs and pick up where the chapter continues. Most of these subjects have really simple explanations. Believe me, I'm no rocket scientist.

Insight will salve your emotions much better than statistics. By understanding the reasoning that goes into how we go about flying, you'll come away with the same realization I made in Junior High: These things are not falling out of the sky daily and that's because they are actually quite safe.

Don't forget to take this book along when you fly should a question arise.

Happy landings…

Ray Stark
September 11th, 2002
Carefree, Arizona

*Travelers are always discoverers, especially those who travel by air. There are no signposts in the sky to show a man has passed that way before. There are no channels marked. The flier breaks each second into new uncharted seas.*

—Anne Morrow Lindbergh (1906-2001) North to the Orient

# Contents

*"If you have knowledge, let others light their candles at it."*

—Margaret Fuller (1810-1850)

# One:

# Fear and Numbers

**By** now you have heard many of the statistics regarding the safety of airline travel. For many people, reconciling the fact that your chances of dying on a commercial airplane flight are nearly the same as being struck by lightning, or scoring a winning lotto ticket, goes a long way to allay the innate fear each of us experience. People are vastly different, and even someone who is rational about most things might find flying in a plane a trigger to the roller coaster ride of irrational fear. This anxiety is not their fault, but simply the way Mother Nature made them.

Some apprehension is normal for any flier. As with any other endeavor, repetition of an experience can remove or reduce apprehension as one builds familiarity. Some people only fly every other year or so. Even those who fly once a month on business find themselves faced with some area of airline travel that generates concern. Many passengers ask the flight crewmembers when a question arises. Some never do. For these apprehensive individuals, there is precious little information available on commercial aviation to help answer the questions nearly every flier has asked at one time or another.

Some passengers are so traumatized by the mere thought of flying that they focus on their fears during the event rather than on how they can resolve them. In over twenty years of flying passengers, I have encountered several travelers that were nearly panic-stricken during a routine flight. Some have bolted off the aircraft as the Flight Attendants prepared to close the door, unable to go through with the

1

flight. Many I have been able to sit with while deadheading on company business have confessed a variety of concerns. I have been able to coax most of these passengers out of their fear for a moment by talking about each phase of the flight, each noise, and the conversations have had a noticeable calming of their fears.

Once I was deadheading in uniform to Albuquerque where I was to start a trip. One lady boarded the aircraft and announced to all within earshot, "I am terrified by flying so I am sitting by that pilot!" I responded, "Lucky me!" I sensed she had a good sense of humor so I played her good nature to my advantage. I got her to look out the window and open up about her fears. She told me her father's sudden illness meant a drive was out of the question and the choice was simple: Fly or not go at all. By the time we touched down in Albuquerque, she was visibly relaxed and, as if an afterthought commented, "Gee, that wasn't so bad. What are you doing in three days when I have to go back home?" Smiling, I responded, "I am sure as heck not going to come out here and get you." She laughed and told me that I had indeed helped her and the information I shared would come in handy on the trip home. I mentioned to her I had given thought to writing this information down and she responded, "I sure wish you would! Your explanation was what I needed to hear." You hold in your hands the product of that chance meeting.

There is nothing worse than dealing with fear punctuated by moments of panic. Often, this fear derives simply from the fact that we are "not in control" as we sit strapped into our passenger seats. This must be the origin of the saying, "Pilots make terrible passengers."

# Pilots Are People Too

Worrying is natural. Fear and worrying are what keep the species alive. Otherwise we would all be bungee jumping and skydiving with our hair on fire. Not to disparage those who like to do these sorts of activities, they are just not for me. I prefer to ride motorcycles. I understand the risks associated with motorcycles and take measures to minimize the risks the best I can. In my own mind, the enjoyment I receive from riding more than makes up for the added risk associated with the hobby.

I don't mind tumbling around the sky, strapped into an airplane doing aerobatics, but put me near a window on the 49th floor of a major high rise, and the height gives me the "willies." I have heard that pilots per capita are, for some reason, more affected by a fear of heights than the general population. Over years of working with pilots from all backgrounds, it seems that is the way *we* are made. Go figure.

When I fly in small planes I am often initially uneasy. I have spent many hours with my father in small Pipers and Cessnas, but in the past 20 years of professional piloting, I have flown with a good friend in a small plane only a dozen or so times. After flying large transport category aircraft for so long, I find the maneuverability and stability of small planes almost startling compared to what I routinely encounter flying airliners. This attitude reminds me of what passengers on my plane experience as I pilot them. What is normal to me on my plane may raise the neck hair on the folks seated in back. To be a compassionate pilot I must remember this fact.

To be a good pilot means more than following a successful take-off with a successful landing. I must strive to operate my aircraft within a small range of smooth control inputs to give the folks in the back, who pay my salary, the best possible ride. When the ride is beyond my control, I have to tell them why and assure them "We'll be OK, what we are experiencing is normal."

Regardless of what technique works for other people, the key is finding one that works for you. For some individuals, information alone is not enough. In the Appendix, I offer some additional resources for people who find "information" alone doesn't abate their fear or panic. As Oprah Winfrey frequently says, "Perfection is a journey, rather than a destination." You may have to work at your fears prior to each flight, perhaps for the rest of your life. Others may find fears put to rest for good. Hopefully, the information provided in this book will help those "nervous fliers" realize the fears and concerns they harbor are normal and have already been addressed by those of us in the aviation system. They were our fears too, but we have learned to deal with them in a way that minimizes their impact.

# Media Conditioning

Many forget the influence the media has upon our determination of risk. In the past, the press occasionally resorted to "creative journalism," ignoring the facts in an attempt to sell papers or snag viewers. I would like to think that compassion for our fellow human in distress is what draws us to these stories, but sometimes I am compelled to think otherwise. The basic fact is: Blood sells. I refer to this peculiar fascination as the "Titanic Syndrome." The public's interest in accidents is normal and natural, as is their natural empathy with those souls facing their certain end. However, I think the media milks these stories in the name of ratings, passing up a great opportunity to educate, and in turn, the media perpetuates the "mystery" that surrounds aviation.

Naturally, in this day and age of instant information, we want immediate answers when, at times, none are available. Television coverage has become so intense, reporter's now camp at the scene of a news event awaiting any shred of newsworthy information. Using the time after an aviation accident to inform and educate about what is normal in aviation helps the public learn. Past accident reports have focused on the aftermath with an apparent aim of quickly solving the accident rather than relaying the facts as they became available. To paraphrase the poet Canby, "Journalists often burst into conclusions at the spark of evidence." Aircraft accident investigations are extremely complex undertakings and initial "explanations" by media representatives or supposed "experts" inevitably prove incorrect. Informed conjecture is fine but must be presented as conjecture, not fact.

Lately there has been great improvement by the press in an attempt to present more of the facts and less of the contrived, "we've already solved this accident" mentality. I hope this trend continues, benefiting society as more passengers, and potential passengers, learn about the aviation system.

Hollywood, on the other hand, has far more license for creativity. Their whole purpose is to entertain, enthrall, and push as many emotional buttons as possible, offering you a "mental vacation" for the time you are seated in the theater. Unfortunately, past movie directors have usually gone for the cheap thrill and avoided all connection with reality when dealing with stories involving aviation. Very few movies make any attempt to depict what a real crew might do in an emergency and fewer still describe a real airplane's actual capabilities. After all this conditioning, I am not surprised some of my passengers expect the worst every time they fly. I hate to make generalizations, but if you forgot everything you learned about aviation from Hollywood, that might be a *good* thing. Hopefully, after reading this book, you'll have a much smaller basis for your fears and concerns.

## The Real Numbers

Here are a few statistics that illustrate the safety of commercial jet travel in a dramatic way.

In 1998 for example, 18 million flights carried 1.3 billion people around the world. That's over three million people in the air per day worldwide. Only ten flights that year ended with fatalities. That means your chances of being involved in a fatal accident are one in three million. To put this into perspective, you'd have to fly once a day for over *8200* years to accumulate three million flights.

The Boeing 737 I fly is the most popular airliner ever produced. At any given time 800 737s are airborne. That is one 737 taking off every six seconds throughout the day and that is just one model of commercial airliner. Counting all the commercial airliners in service throughout the world, an aircraft takes off roughly every second of the day.

Compared to driving, flying in a commercial jet airliner is 22 times safer. In fact, all the people killed *worldwide* in jet accidents over the past 40 years roughly equals the number of people killed on U.S. highways in a six-month period. Even more amazing is the fact that more people die in a three-month period on U.S. highways than have died in the 60 years on American commercial flights. These highway deaths, no less sad than any others, rarely make the news. Society has come to accept this daily carnage on the highways. However, let any death occur from aviation related causes and you can be sure this accident will make headlines. Aviation accidents are partly newsworthy simply because they are so *rare*.

Enough numbers. Now let us turn our attention to the people behind the scenes who design and operate the planes as well as those who operate the system the planes fly within—the Air Traffic Control (ATC) system.

# Two:
# The Machine

**In** the early days of aviation (only about 70 years ago), the concept of hiring someone to take you, by airplane, where you wanted to go was one of the first practical uses of multi-seat aircraft. In the beginning, you sat in an open cockpit plane with 80 mile per hour winds blowing by, in all sorts of weather. These planes were made of wooden sticks and were covered with cotton fabric, which was covered with "dope," (a paint-like material that made the cotton much stronger as well as waterproof).

Improvements in design moved the fare-paying passengers inside, but for a while, left the pilots out in the cold in open cockpits. Soon, improvements in making lighter, stronger metals, led to the first all-metal airplane. Engineers discovered that, by combining lightweight aluminum with other compounds, they greatly increased the strength of the resulting metal with little additional weight. This metallurgical knowledge, coupled with improvements in engine technology, allowed very reliable and capable aircraft to be pressed into service. That said, even the aircraft designers were unsure that six or eight people could be found who wanted to fly to the same destination on the same day. No one anticipated the demand we see today.

The Douglas DC-3 was one of the first modern aircraft to fly the skies in the name of commerce, hauling both passengers and freight great distances with excellent reliability. This plane was so well designed that many are still in use today, some 65 years after the first one rolled off the assembly line (See Figure 1).

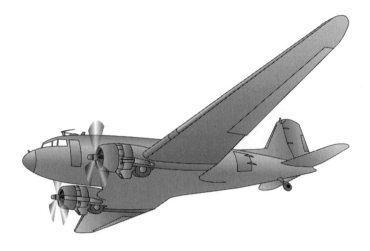

*Figure 1. Douglas DC 3*

Today's modern jet aircraft has many similarities with the venerable old DC-3. They are made of virtually the same metal and held together by thousands of rivets, nearly each one set in place by hand. But what we have learned over the past 65 years has led aircraft designers to add a whole host of safety features.

Many of the systems on the older planes have been simplified or vastly improved. For example, a hydraulic pump that used to last several hundred hours between failures now lasts many thousands of hours. Airplanes are very expensive to operate and maintain. Cost as well as safety has driven this improvement in reliability. The less often planes break down, the less they have to be taken out of service to be fixed. An aircraft manufacturer's prime sales assets are reliability and safety. They go hand-in-hand. No airline wants to spend millions of dollars on an aircraft that breaks down frequently. So, for safety and reliability, many systems are built with "redundancy." In other words, they have a back-up system or in some cases, two or more. Take the Boeing 737 hydraulic system for example. Without getting too technical, this system primarily operates the flight controls, the raising of the landing gear, the thrust reversers (the sliding sleeves that divert airflow forward to slow the plane on landing), and supplies power to the brake system. To do this, Boeing has created the A and B systems as mirror hydraulic systems, each independently capable of doing the job without any help from the other. If any part of the system breaks down, the remaining systems carry the load.

## Extra Technical Stuff For Those Who Want To Know

*Each hydraulic system gets its power from two pumps. In the 737, the A system engine driven pump is mounted directly on the engine accessory drive and is powered by the number 1 engine (like the power steering pump on your car). The other pump is operated by an electric motor. The electrical power for that pump is produced by a generator on the number 2 engine. That way, in the event that the number one engine fails, at least one pump remains operating (the electric pump powered by the number 2 engine). The B Hydraulic system is exactly opposite with the number 2 engine driving a pump as well as the number 1 engine supplying electrical power for the electric B pump. Without this simple design feature, a simple engine failure would also mean a hydraulic failure. With this design architecture, lose any major component (engine, generator, engine driven or electrical hydraulic pump) and you have not lost a single hydraulically powered item. Things hum along normally. The thoughtful engineers at Boeing have tried to plan for every eventuality.*

*Just in case, they have provided yet another smaller, totally independent, back-up system for the rudder and thrust reversers. This system is known as the Standby system and it enables the pilots to fly the plane if some unforeseen failure has occurred to both the A and B systems, a very unlikely occurrence (See Figure 2).*

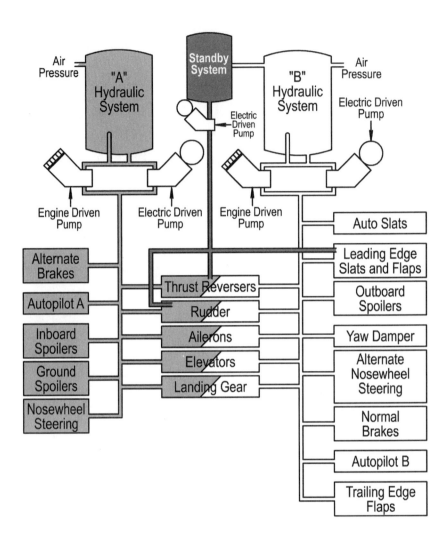

*Figure 2. Hydraulic Systems*

The Boeing 737 is very capable of being landed with no hydraulic system at all. Each flight control, (rudder, ailerons, and elevator) is controlled by cables that go to the yoke (steering wheel) and rudder pedals in front of the pilot. Like your car's power steering, the power assist is nice to have, but the plane can be flown and landed without any hydraulic power at all should the need arise. Most commercial aircraft have these cables to the major flight controls, as yet *another* back up. Even the landing gear is designed to free-fall into position without any hydraulic assistance.

In addition to basic aircraft system improvements, new technology has led to installation of safety enhancements unthought of only a decade ago. A device called a Ground Proximity Warning Systems (GPWS) was installed in the early 1970s. This system would alert the pilots if mountains were approaching, or if the aircraft was descending into flat terrain. This terrain warning system relied on a weak radar beam looking little more than a mile or so ahead of the aircraft. Based on then-current technology (radar), the system was very limited in its ability to adequately warn pilots they were approaching terrain. But, it was a vast improvement over no warning system at all.

Now, as the result of the new technology and the creation of the Global Positioning Satellite System (GPS), exact locations to within feet can be determined anywhere on the globe or inflight. In concert with this technology, a computer database of all high terrain across the entire globe can be maintained on a CD-ROM. By knowing the location of the aircraft with a very high degree of precision (based on GPS position information) and comparing that to known areas of high terrain (from the world terrain map on CD-ROM which has been made possible by very accurate photos taken from the Space Shuttle), pilots can be warned well in advance of the threat of high terrain ahead of their aircraft. For example, imagine if a computer knew where every item of furniture was located in your house and could warn you of objects in your path as you walked blindfolded from one room to another. "Controlled flight into terrain," or in other words, allowing a plane that is functioning perfectly fine to fly into the ground, is a leading cause of aviation accidents. A recent report indicates that, since the EGPWS system was introduced, no aircraft with the EGPWS system has been involved with any controlled flight into terrain accidents. Improvements in technology have made a previous aircraft system many times more effective. This greatly enhances safety.

Another improvement aimed at preventing airborne collisions is the Traffic alert and Collision Avoidance System (TCAS) (See Figure 3). The TCAS displays to the pilot of a TCAS equipped aircraft the location and altitude of other aircraft that are equipped with an operating transponder. The TCAS will issue avoidance maneuver commands to both offending planes to avoid a collision. Transponders are devices that radio essentially a unique code number representing one aircraft to ATC. This code shows up on their radarscope like a license plate on an automobile, and ensures each aircraft on the radarscope is correctly identified. An operating transponder is required for entry into most controlled airspace.

Other systems that look ahead for dangerous wind conditions called "wind shear" help protect aircraft on approach or while taking off, the most vulnerable times for wind shear encounters. (For a detailed description of wind shear, see Chapter 8, "Aviation Weather.) Radar improvements both in the cockpit and on the ground have enabled marked improvements in identifying dangerous weather. Fire suppression systems installed on aircraft have protected against fires in lavatory garbage cans and in baggage holds, both places where fires have led to loss of life. In fact, the move to larger two-engine aircraft has been a safety move. Statistically, the more engines you have the more chance you have for a failure. New system improvements are on the drawing boards to make flying even safer in the future.

## "Mother, May I...."

With so many levels of redundancy, the Federal Aviation Administration allows each type of aircraft to operate with a few systems degraded. A book called the Minimum Equipment List (MEL) is a very careful and cautious list, born of experience, identifying things that may be allowed to be inoperative but which do not affect aircraft safety.

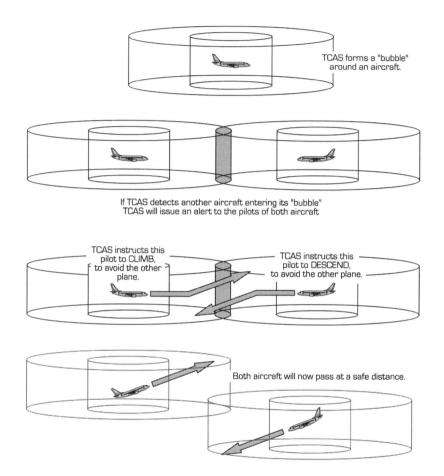

*Figure 3. TCAS*

▼ From the Master Minimum Equipment List published by the Federal Aviation Administration (FAA):

*"The FAR (Federal Aviation Regulations) require that all equipment installed on an aircraft in compliance with airworthiness standards and the Operating Rules must be operative. However, the rules also permit the publication of a Minimum Equipment List (MEL) where compliance with certain equipment requirements is*

*not necessary in the interest of safety under all operating conditions. Experience has shown that with the various levels of redundancy designed into aircraft, operation of every system or installed component may not be necessary when the remaining operative equipment can provide an acceptable level of safety. A Master Minimum Equipment List (MMEL) is developed by the FAA, with participation by the aviation industry, to improve aircraft utilization and therefore provide more convenient and economical air transportation for the public.*

▼ *The MEL does not contain obviously required items such as wings, flaps and rudders.*

▼ *The MEL is intended to permit operation with inoperative items of equipment for a period of time until repairs can be accomplished."*

From this Master MEL each airline builds a MEL for each specific aircraft type, identifying what equipment can be inoperative and what restrictions, if any, are imposed on the flight as a result.

As we discussed earlier, many systems are so "backed up" by design that it is perfectly safe to fly without all the parts working. Often, the MEL specifies restrictions that eliminate potential problems. For example, if the weather radar fails, as long as the flight is clear of any thunderstorm activity, the aircraft is cleared to depart. If weather conditions are such that the weather radar is needed to fly this leg, the radar will have to be fixed before departure.

Say for example, you have a landing light out. Should an aircraft be grounded or take a delay in order to replace a burned out landing light bulb when the flight is scheduled to operate in daylight conditions? Even at night, most aircraft have several forward facing lights, which provide more than adequate lighting when one or two "headlights" are burned out. In this example, the MEL allows the flight to continue provided that the landing light is replaced on the next pass through a city with maintenance technicians. More important items must be fixed before flying resumes. If the MEL does not specifically say you can go with a broken item—YOUR PLANE IS GROUNDED.

Regarding maintenance, airlines have mechanics and spare parts at designated locations called "maintenance bases." These locations are like a car dealerships. They have trained personnel experienced in every intimate detail of the aircraft that their company operates, and they have nearly every part necessary to get a plane fixed, and on its way. Obviously, these maintenance bases are expensive and having airline maintenance personnel at every city the airline serves is neither economically feasible nor necessary. But nearly every location the airline serves has some maintenance available, sometimes known as "contract maintenance."

The term "contract" derives the name from the fact that, though the maintenance individuals are not employed by the airline, they have been certified for airline category maintenance by the FAA, and have passed standards set by the airline. In other words, the maintenance personnel are under contract to the airline when the need for maintenance arises.

Contract maintenance may be personnel from another airline who may work on the very same model aircraft or other aircraft by the same manufacturer, or perhaps other manufacturers altogether. Let's say an American 737 has a maintenance problem at San Francisco International. The contract maintenance technicians might be from United Airlines, which also operates Boeing 737s. The experienced United mechanics lend a set of qualified eyes to the American head mechanics located at their maintenance headquarters in Tulsa. If necessary, the United mechanics will be faxed detailed Boeing instructions for troubleshooting a problem or determining what action to take, just like the instructions American mechanics use.

On another day, a United jet may receive attention in an American maintenance location by an American mechanic. When dealing with safety, the name of the airline on the tail of the jet is of little importance. The signature of the mechanic places his or her reputation and livelihood on the line, as each is ultimately held responsible by the FAA for the quality of the work they perform. Aviation maintenance personnel are very responsible and dedicated people who are very picky about doing the job right—the first time.

# Time To Fly!

You may be surprised by the fact that airplanes like to fly. They don't like to sit around for long periods. Machines tend to work more reliably the more frequently they are used. The average airliner flies about eight to ten hours per day. In addition to time spent in the air, the plane sits at the gate before or between flights another two to three hours or more throughout the day with many systems operating.

The Boeing 737 is the most popular airliner ever produced. I have flown this Boeing for over 20 years and I say with affection and admiration, the 737 is truly a wonderful plane. I liken this jet to the Chevrolet Caprice taxicabs you see all over the country. They are everywhere. Unlike the Chevy that went out of production as other models came off the line, Boeing has refined and modernized the 737 since the aircraft first flew in the mid-sixties. While the older ones closely resemble the newer models, they actually share very few parts. Their popularity stems from the fact that they are safe, reliable, and economical planes that can do just about anything you ask of them. Surely, in 65 years, this aircraft will be thought of as the DC-3 of the jet age. (See Figure 4)

*Figure 4. Boeing 737*

# Boeing 737 Trivia

More Boeing 737 airliners have been produced than any other airliner in history.

**First flown:** 1967

**Number produced:** 4,000 in service with nearly 1,500 on order from the factory

**Empty weight:** About 65,000 lbs (32 tons, no fuel or passengers on board)

**Maximum take-off weight:** 150,000 lbs (75 tons fully loaded)

Take-off speed: Lightly loaded 125mph, heavyweight 170 mph

**Landing speed:** Lightly loaded 120 mph, heavyweight 140 mph

**Service ceiling (highest altitude flown):** 37,000 feet (41,000 new 700/800 /900 model)

**Maximum speed:** About 590 miles per hour (not counting head/ tailwind affects)

**Range:** Usually about 2,500 miles with some models configured to go anywhere in the world with only one gas stop

Fuel burn taxiing out: About 200 gallons per hour

**Fuel burn at brake release (take-off):** As high as 2,500 gallons per hour (125 average car gas tanks!)

Tire life: About 45 landings and then tires are sent off for retreading. Airliner tires are made extra strong and each is designed to have new tread applied after its old tread is worn off. Landing burns off considerable tread and produces the blue smoke seen just as the aircraft touches down. Each tire can be retreaded up to six times before being retired. During the summer months due to heat stress, the tire is only retreaded four times before it is junked. Often tires past their useful life are used on the jetways that passengers walk down to board the plane. Each main tire has 26 plies or "belts" for added strength. (The average car tire has 4.)

**Total weight of the paint on the outside of the jet:** About 200 lbs, depending on livery (company paint design)

# General Aircraft Stability

Aircraft, with a few exceptions, (fighter aircraft and the Space Shuttle) are designed to be stable in flight. This means they continue to travel along smoothly, but if bumped or jostled either by outside forces (wind currents) or the pilot's inputs to the controls, they eventually return to the equilibrium state they were at before. How they do this is a reflection on the clever engineers who have perfected the machines that carry us into the sky. For more technical reasons, see the end of this chapter.

So far, we've looked at a well-manufactured machine that has been designed to meet the needs of the airlines in terms of capacity, reliability, and safety, and which also incorporates a multitude of improvements over previous models. But how about the one you are flying on right now? How do you know that sound you just heard is a good sound? In the next chapter let's examine what sounds and smells you might expect to encounter in a routine flight.

## Technical Stuff

*Why planes are stable in flight. (Or, "Things I have learned about aircraft by building and flying model planes over 45 years." Model planes must obey the same laws of full size aircraft. They don't have the advantage of a pilot to correct for weaknesses in design.) First a definition of the term "stability":*

*From* The American Heritage Dictionary: *Stability— resistance to sudden change, dislodgment or overthrow.*

*First, to ensure an aircraft is stable, the* **Center of Gravity** *of the aircraft has to be in front of the* **Center of Lift**. *Imagine an arrow shaft without tail feathers, or a weighted end (See Figure 5a). If you threw this shaft, it would tumble through the air demonstrating little or no stability. Stick a weight on one end of the shaft, and*

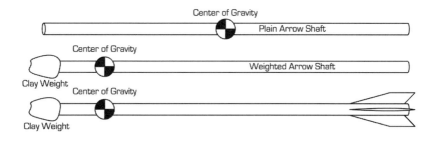

*Figure 5a. Center of Gravity*

suddenly the shaft follows the heavy end when tossed. Still the shaft wobbles around somewhat in flight, so stabilizing tail feathers are added. Each of these tail feathers is a small **airfoil**. Airfoils generate lift when immersed in moving air at a slight angle. The lift they produce returns the airfoil (and the shaft they are attached to) to zero angle relative to the air (this angle is called **Angle of Attack**). This is why arrows fly so wonderfully straight and true. This is the reason planes have tail "feathers" called **stabilizers** located in the rear of the fuselage. These keep the plane going smoothly in one direction.

Lift is generated by the wing airfoil as it meets the wind at an angle. This is why you see jetliners racing down the runway on take-off—"rotating." By changing the angle of the wing in the flow of air (Angle of Attack), the wing produces lift. This lift raises the plane skyward. Upon landing, the nose of the plane settles to the runway and most of the lift is lost. (See Figure 5b)

Just as in balance, where the total weight of an item is focused at one point near its middle, a wing has a Center of Lift where the lifting force balances or focuses. By placing this Center of Lift behind the Center of Gravity (CG), lift produced will not interfere with the stability of the plane as it moves through the air. Were the Center of Lift

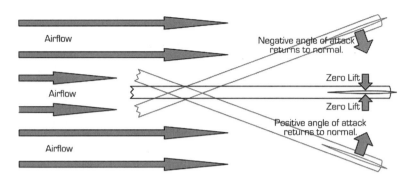

Airflow

Airflow

Airflow

Negative angle of attack returns to normal.

Zero Lift

Zero Lift

Positive angle of attack returns to normal.

*Figure 5b.*

placed in front of the Center of Gravity, it would force the craft in different directions depending on the amount of lift. (Imagine our arrow shaft trying to fly backwards through the air.) This is what engineers call "unstable." Placing the Center of Gravity in front of the Center of Lift, means the plane will keep going in a stable direction regardless of lift (much like the weighted arrow shaft). This is why many paper airplanes don't fly very well. After explaining this concept to my daughter's eighth grade class, the kids were able to identify why their paper planes flew poorly and what to do to make them fly better. The results were dramatic. A simple concept, but absolutely essential if the aircraft is to fly unaided.

Some aircraft violate this rule when it is to their advantage. Many fighter aircraft have their Center of Gravity behind their Center of Lift because this makes the aircraft turn quicker in combat. The only thing that makes this type aircraft controllable is constant correction by the flight control computer. Without this computer help, the aircraft would be uncontrollable by the pilot alone. Imagine an arrow flying through the air backwards, constantly being prevented from swapping ends because an onboard computer is constantly moving the

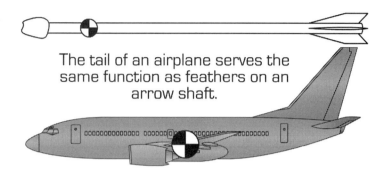

The tail of an airplane serves the same function as feathers on an arrow shaft.

*Figure 5c.*

tail fins. No human pilot alone could react fast enough. The Space Shuttle also has a slightly aft CG and relies on computers for control.

My point here is simply that while experiencing turbulence, you shouldn't worry about the aircraft "going out of control." The aircraft is designed to recover from an upset like turbulence. Just make sure you are seated and your seatbelt is fastened. You may be startled by a sudden bump or drop but you will come through just fine. Just imagine how bumpy a car would be if you were driving down the Interstate at 500 miles per hour!

21

*"Stress is an ignorant state.*
*It believes that everything is an emergency."*

Natalie Goldberg, *Wild Mind (1990)*

# Three:

## What's That Noise?

### Things That Go "Bump" In the Flight

**Many** passengers tell me they rely on the facial expressions of the Flight Attendants and other passengers to know if things are going OK. After reading this chapter you will know more about what is normal than many experienced Flight Attendants.

### Where To Sit?

A question crewmembers frequently get asked by passengers during boarding is, "Where is the best place to sit?" Statistically, there is actually no basis for saying that sitting in any one section is safer than another. I prefer any window seat from the front door to the over wing exit. The closer to any exit, the better. The ride is quieter and generally smoother toward the front of the aircraft. (For the reason, see Chapter 9, "Aerospace Physiology.") Where you sit on a plane determines what noises you hear and how loud they are.

### At the Gate

When the plane is parked at the gate the situation reminds me of a patient in the operating room: all the doctors and staff are doing things in concert with each other but with an independent focus as well. Ground crewmembers are plugging in lavatory drain carts and draining and replenishing fluids and the fueler is hooking up hoses to refuel the thousands of gallons necessary for the next flight. The apparent chaos is actually a very carefully choreographed dance. The baggage handlers are opening the baggage bins under the floor ("THUNK") and you can hear them "carefully" handling your prized new bag ("WHUMP—THUD"). I still laugh when I think of a friend's announcement to the passengers about a slight delay, "Folks, the machine that rips the handle off your suitcase and tears your bag is broken so we're having to do that by hand today. Loading up is taking a bit longer but we'll be under way shortly." He was kidding of course. In reality, the baggage handlers are working in a hot, cramped room, often only about four feet high, on knee pads, trying to move bags that sometime weigh half as much as they do. Today, many baggage handlers are women. The "rampers," as they are called, do a super job considering the stress of the working conditions and time limits under which they operate.

Up near the front of the plane you may hear a crunching or banging sound as the ground crew hooks up the tow bar that connects the pushback tug to the aircraft. During pushback this small metal tube will bear the full brunt of the pressure as the powerful tug labors to move the plane. Medium size airliners like Boeing 737s can weigh upwards of 150,000 lbs (75 tons) when fully loaded. Boeing 747s and other jumbos can weigh nearly a million pounds (500 tons).

From the cockpit, you may hear audio warnings as the flight crew tests some of the avionics during their pre-flight. ("Whoop-whoop—PULL UP—PULL UP! WIND SHEAR! WIND SHEAR!") If seated near the wing you may hear the hydraulic pumps sing out as they are tested. Just before engine start, they come on with a solid note in preparation for pushback from the gate.

As you board, you may notice fog coming out of the ceiling or air vents over the seats. This occurs in the summer in humid areas of the country, and is the very cold air from the air conditioning system interacting with the humid air in the cabin. (See Chapter 8, "Aviation Weather" for an explanation of why fog forms.) If your aircraft has been on the ground for some time, condensation may start dripping from those vents.

If seated near a galley, you'll hear provisioners and their trucks restocking the galleys with ice, food, and canned goods. The beer kits are like heavy aluminum industrial strength coolers and they get slammed in and out of the galley racks.

# Smells

You may smell the strong odor of coffee from coffee makers in the galleys. Sometimes the hot plates on the coffee makers burn off yesterday's spilled coffee and put out a strong smell.

On a cold morning, the heaters may be running full blast and a faint smell like burning plastic may be in the air. The heater ducts are made of fiberglass and, when at high temperature, they may give off a faint "burning wire" smell. This is normal too.

Another smell you may come across in winter is the smell of de-ice fluid. This is the sticky fluid de-ice crews spray on the outside of the plane to melt off any accumulated ice. This fluid is sprayed on hot and smells very sweet, like baking cookies. This smell can stay with the plane for a week or more and can often be first smelled around the entry door areas during boarding, where the fluid has collected near the door seal area. If you are onboard as the plane is de-iced, the smell will be most noticeable as the air conditioning system is turned back on. Occasionally a little of the fluid or fog is drawn into the air conditioning bays under the fuselage, and a very noticeable wisp of what appears to be white smoke, may spill from the overhead air vents. Not to worry, the smell will dissipate quickly.

# Engine Start

Once the passengers are seated and their bags stowed, the plane is ready for engine start. This is usually done while the plane is being pushed out of the gate. Occasionally, the Auxiliary Power Unit (APU) may be inoperative and the aircraft engines will be started at the gate, using ground power. The APU is a little jet engine in the tail that operates an electrical generator for lights, while the main engine driven generators are off at the gate. You may see the cabin lights flash as the pilots switch electrical power sources. This is normal. The APU also provides the pneumatic air pressure to start the engines.

> *Note: The FAA will not allow a commercial airliner to move while passengers are standing. If you jump up to get something out of the overhead bin or switch seats, you will delay the pushback, and may possibly delay the arrival of the plane significantly if Ground Control holds the aircraft at the gate. Standing after the plane has begun movement during pushback will bring the plane to a quick halt. Stay seated at all times until the pilots turn off the overhead seatbelt sign, inflight! The same holds true for jumping up to get your bag after landing. Remain seated until the fasten seatbelt sign has been turned off.*

The APU that supplies electrical power to the cabin lighting also provides pneumatic air to power the air conditioning systems. As the engines begin to start, you will notice the plane gets slightly quieter. This is due to the fact that the APU on most aircraft cannot power the air conditioning/heating system, and supply air to the engine starters simultaneously. The heating/cooling units or "packs" are turned off just prior to engine start. This is why the cabin gets warm during engine start during the summer as the air conditioning is momentarily turned off. As the engines wind up, you may hear a low throbbing sound that is interrupted after awhile by the sound of the engines lighting off. Often this produces a deeper tone that slowly winds up to the usual "vacuum cleaner" sound that jet engines so closely mimic.

For those seated behind a jet motor during start, you may see a cloud of smoke pouring out of the tail, usually on cold mornings. This is unburned fuel vapor that has not yet ignited. Just like your car on a cold morning, it takes a minute to get the fire burning in "all cylinders," so to speak. Once the fire in the engine spreads to the entire circumference of the combustion chamber, the smoke diminishes rapidly. You may smell some of this smoke as the air conditioning packs suck the fumes in after engine start.

A much more rare event during engine start is seeing a "fireball" or flash roll out the tail of the motor. If, as on a cold day, the motors spark plugs fail to ignite the cold fuel vapor, after a short while, the Captain will discontinue the start attempt and will motor (spin) the engine to dissipate the remaining vapor in preparation for another start attempt. Often a breeze blowing at right angles or into the tail of the motor can prohibit normal light off.

During the restart, a small amount of fuel pooled in the combustion chamber may ignite and be blown out the tailpipe during engine start. This is a rare occurrence on more modern engines but it still happens on occasion. This is OK. Fires inside your engine are good things to have. That is the *only* place you want to have fire on an aircraft.

> *Hint: If you are flying at night, watch for other planes as yours taxies out to the runway. Boeing 737s exhibit a red "glow" from the back of the motors due to the thousand degree heat generated in the engines at idle thrust. You can see this glow quite clearly from the rear.*

## Taxi Out

Once the jet is pushed back far enough to clear ground equipment at the gate, and once the motors are started and engine generators placed on-line (another lighting flicker in the cabin), the plane is ready to taxi out for take-off.

Shortly after the plane begins to move, if you are seated near the wing, you may hear the flap motor running the flaps down to the take-off position. ("mMMRRrrRRrrRR" The noise reminds me of a giant electric can opener.) This motor is hydraulic, and is the second most noticeable sound inflight (after the landing gear going down "CLUNK–SHEUSSHHHH" just prior to landing).

As you taxi, you may hear groaning coming from the brakes located on the main landing gear. Just like car brakes that "squeal" a bit when applied, airliner brakes "hum" or "sing" but, at a lower frequency, because of the extra mass of the brake assembly. A car has only one disc per wheel whereas aircraft brakes are comprised of four or more discs per wheel. You'll notice this noise particularly just as the plane comes to a stop. Another good reason to sit in a window seat; you know what the plane is doing.

Occasionally, if you are seated up front, you may hear or feel the front nose strut. A strut is basically a big shock absorber that is part of the nose landing gear. When struts are cold, as the plane begins to build up taxi speed, the front of the plane will ride like it has "square tires." Cold tires can develop a temporary flat spot after parking overnight, which disappears once the tire warms up. This bounciness will go away once the plane speeds past the point of harmonics and the front strut warms up. For a minute though, the ride feels like there is something wrong with the wheels. This usually occurs on the first flight of the day, most often in cold weather.

For those seated near the lavatories, you may hear the slam of a toilet seat as the plane taxis out. Believe it or not, at the request of some customers, Boeing has installed hydraulic dampers on the toilet seats on the 777 aircraft so they don't slam but rather close gently if left up during taxi. Technology at its finest.

Another *noise* you will hear is the Flight Attendant Safety Briefing. This is an FAA mandatory briefing required before every flight and it is important that you listen carefully. This briefing contains critical information unique to the plane you are on. Many frequent flyers can recite this briefing by heart, and to them, it probably is noise. The briefing is very important for new fliers, because it details important things like where exits are and what to do in the event the aircraft loses pressurization. A yawner. Been there, done that. See Chapter 6, "When Things Go Wrong."

Occasionally, you may notice a screw missing from a panel out on the wing or on a part of the engine or engine pylon. Not to worry. Aircraft manufacturers put extra screws on each panel to account for the occasional screw that backs out as a result of the vibrations encountered in flight. Feel free to mention the condition to a crewmember so it can be taken care of, but don't worry about something happening as the panel is unlikely to fall off. In fact, many of the panels on the plane are not even required for flight, and are allowed to be missing in accordance with the MEL (Minimum Equipment List). If you notice one missing you can ask a Flight Attendant to check with the pilot. If I fly an aircraft with a panel that has been removed by maintenance and the panel is in an area that might be seen by passengers, I brief the Flight Attendants so they are aware should any passenger notice.

# Take-off

As the plane is cleared onto the runway, the pilots signal the Flight Attendants either with a verbal announcement or a "ding-dong" over the P.A. system. The Flight Attendants usually make the "We've been cleared for take-off" announcement, which may not actually be true. Sometimes the pilots are cleared onto the runway and held while some other traffic clears ahead or departs a crossing runway. Sometimes plans change and the tower controllers cancel your clearance to take the runway or take-off. As far as the Flight Attendants know though, the pilots have signaled them, "We are going *soon*."

When the Captain lines up with the runway, you may hear the whine of the tires on the rain grooves cut into the runway to aid in braking traction, like on the freeway, only across the runway rather than parallel with it. Once cleared for take-off, you will hear the powerful roar of the engines increase until they all stabilize. Engines, like people, have personalities and some accelerate slower at first than others. This is normal. Once they all assume the same mid power setting, the pilot performing the take-off pushes them up to take-off power, and you are off and running!

While the aircraft accelerates down the runway, you may feel the airplane bouncing if the runway is not perfectly level. Few are, and bumps and bounces are normal. Sometimes they cause a "BANG" as a pavement joint slams the landing gear. Runway lights marking the centerline of the runway are housed in little metal bumps, like the ceramic dots forming the lane boundaries on the highway. You may hear their pounding noise increasing in frequency as you accelerate.

Remember, the plane weighs upwards of 50 tons and just before liftoff, it is rolling along the runway at 120-160 miles per hour or more. Until the plane starts to rotate the nose up, it's just a bus with wings. Once the "angle of attack" (or angle of the wing relative to the wind) increases enough for the wings to create lift equal to the weight of the plane, only then does the plane rise free from the earth, the wheels now useless (see Figure 6).

If you are seated behind the wing and if you listen very carefully just as the plane lifts off, you can hear the roar of the jet engines diminish slightly as the plane flies away from the ground. The reflected noise from the motors no longer bounces off the runway and back into the plane as it climbs out.

Up front, you may hear the nose wheels quickly winding down during retraction as they come in contact with "snubbers" that press against the fast-spinning tires to stop them from spinning in the nose wheel well. The brakes stop the main-gear tires rotation during the retraction sequence. The nose wheels have no brakes and rely on the "snubbers" which are heavy asbestos pads on spring arms. Sometimes nose tires out of balance will vibrate noticeably during retraction, shaking the front end of the plane very slightly, but this is

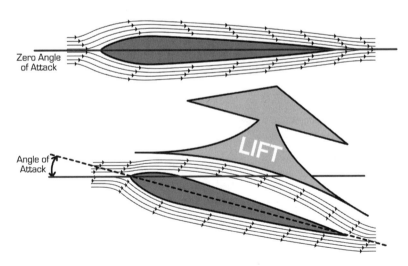

*Figure 6. Angle of Attack*

normal and the pilots will probably get new tires mounted on the next pass through a maintenance base. Tires get replaced about every other week on the average jetliner. This short life is why aircraft tires are designed to be retreaded and used more than once.

In the middle to rear of the cabin, you'll notice once the landing gear is raised, the plane gets quieter. Sometimes one main gear will beat the other to the up position and the plane will "kick" slightly from one side to the other as the airflow beneath the plane is momentarily disturbed. Passing air disturbed by the landing gear bumps against the tail due to the high pitch angle during take-off. This turbulence generated by the landing gear is what makes the characteristic sound when the landing gear is lowered. During take-off the engines drown out the gear noise but during landing the engines are at a reduced power setting and the gear noise is very noticeable.

Thirty seconds or so after take-off, you'll hear Mr. Flap Motor singing as he brings the flaps up to the stowed position. From that point on, all will be fairly quiet except for the engines speeding up and down as the plane levels off from time to time en route to cruise altitude.

Occasionally, if your plane is fully loaded during the hotter time of year, you'll hear the air conditioning being reset. During extremely heavyweight take-offs, the air conditioning duties are given to the APU to allow the entire engine thrust to contribute towards getting the aircraft airborne. Once airborne, and usually right after the flaps come up, the engines once again resume the duty of powering the A/C packs and the APU is shutdown. You may sense a surge of air out of your overhead vent as this is done.

You may encounter a startling rolling-bumping sensation shortly after take-off. This is the disturbed air from the plane that departed just ahead of yours. Off each wing tip grows a vortex of wind, similar to a miniature horizontal tornado (See Figure 7). These vortexes present no real problem to the pilots of a similar sized aircraft other than the uncomfortable surprise of a bump or two, and for this reason, pilots try various techniques to avoid them. Larger planes produce larger vortices than smaller jets, and for that reason, smaller planes

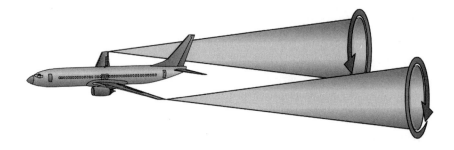

*Figure 7. Wake Vortices*

will delay their take-off until the larger plane ahead is a safe distance away.

> **Hint:** *Up high at cruise altitude you may see other planes passing by. If conditions are right for contrails, you may see the white ice particles forming from the moisture produced by the engine exhaust—like a car on a cold day. If you pass close enough and watch very closely, you can actually see the wing tip vortices whip the engine exhaust into what appear to be rapidly rotating spirals of smoke. This smoke is actually frozen water vapor from the engines. These are the contrails that look like thin white lines in the sky when viewed from the ground. If you watch very closely, you may be able to see these tornados of air spinning very quickly then slowing as they expand.*

If you walk by, or are seated near a door or emergency exit hatch, you may hear a hissing noise, occasionally in the form of a high pitch squeal, which is air leaking out of the plane around a leaky exit seal. These seals are very sturdy rubber and as time goes on they get worn, dusty, and occasionally torn. As a result, they begin to leak. This is normal and when it gets too loud, we have maintenance either clean the seal, or replace it if damaged or worn too much. Don't be concerned about the bad seal causing the door to open or suggesting that the door is not closed all the way. The pilots have DOOR CLOSED lights for every door in the plane to make sure they are in the correct position before pushback from the gate. Even before take-off, the pressurization begins to apply pressure on the door and seal. Often, right after take-off, they will squeal like "piggies" or whistle like a partially open car window. This noise may get louder and louder as you climb, until the pressurization puts enough pressure on the rubber seal and finally stops the squealing. The pressurization system has sufficient additional capacity to pressurize the plane even when a few seals leak. (Read more about the pressure holding the doors closed at altitude in Chapter 9, "Aerospace Physiology.")

## Shhhhhhhhh!

If you fly out of John Wayne Airport in Orange County, CA, you will experience an aggressive noise abatement departure. Due to severe noise restrictions imposed by local authorities, the airport authorities, in cooperation with the FAA, have prescribed a thrust cutback procedure more complicated than most. To minimize noise impact to the neighboring communities, the crew climbs as steeply and as quickly as possible, to 1,200 feet above the ground, where the engines are quickly throttled back to a whisper. The plane then flies a tightly prescribed course over ground-based microphones hooked to a computer. If the pilots violate the noise limits, fines may be imposed on the airline. From a passenger perspective, at cutback your first impression is that both engines have just failed.

Noise abatement departures are quite common now across the country, though normally nowhere near as complicated as in Orange County. Because of the unusual nature of the Orange County departure, most airlines make an announcement to the passengers prior to departure warning them in advance. At most other airports, you would never notice most noise abatement departures, as they are nowhere near as abrupt. While many citizens want convenient access to airports ("Just not in my backyard!"), communities cannot, in and of their own desires, implement noise abatement procedures. This is something handled by the FAA. However, more communities are considering Orange County's approach.

## More Noises

One other noise you may hear on departure, or really at any phase of flight, is weather around the plane. Heavy or frozen rain (light hail) can make a noticeable noise when it hits the outer skin of the plane and can pass so quickly it sounds like a "crack" or "bang". Usually this noise is only heard in the front of the cabin. The noise is *really* loud in the cockpit as it strikes the front windows.

If you are on a propeller commuter aircraft, you may hear ice striking the aircraft as it is shed off the propellers. The propellers have heated blades and the pilots can turn them on when conditions warrant. The ice strikes the fuselage so hard that aircraft manufacturers install sheets of armor adjacent to propellers to prevent the ice from damaging the outer surface of the fuselage.

Another much more rare sound is a "static discharge," where a big spark jumps off the plane, just like a spark jumps off your hand when you reach for some metal object, like a hand rail after dragging your slippered feet on the carpet in the winter. This is normal and usually happens without being heard. Occasionally, when conditions are just right, the spark is so big it departs the plane like a thunderclap. Depending where the spark departs the plane, you may see the bright flash. Generally, the radome, the forward most portion of the nose, is where the energy departs the aircraft. Frequently, in the cockpit, the noise sounds like a shotgun being fired and is heard by passengers seated as far back as the wing. In one instance, I saw the conditions were right for a possible discharge and advised my new First Officer to be ready should a discharge occur. Forty five seconds later came the "BANG" and it instantly got his attention. No big deal. The stray voltage didn't bother the plane at all as the engineers designed systems into the aircraft to deal with just such an occurrence.

## Technical Stuff:

*If you notice along the rear edge of the wingtips and tips of the vertical and horizontal stabilizers there are little "thingies" that stick out (See Figure 8). These are called static wicks. Their job is to take the energy accumulated as the plane flies through certain climactic conditions, which add static energy to the airframe, and release that static energy back into the atmosphere. They do a wonderful job most of the time but on occasion the plane picks up more stray electrons than the static wicks can get rid of. That is when a static discharge occurs. Static discharges almost always occur while flying in clouds.*

Occasionally, airplanes flying well clear of a thunderstorm will get zapped with a lightning bolt. Unlike a static discharge, where the lightning bolt jumps *off* the plane, the lightning bolt is energy jumping *onto* the plane. If a car is a safe place to get struck by lightning because you are insulated from the ground by the rubber tires, a plane must be better yet because you aren't even on the ground. Usually, neither a static discharge nor a lightning bolt has any affect on the plane at all, except where lightning sears off the paint.

You can tell if a plane has been struck by lightning. Those that have usually display a series of zap marks where the paint has been scorched, (usually covered by touch-up paint) often a couple feet above the windows extending the length of the plane. In these areas,

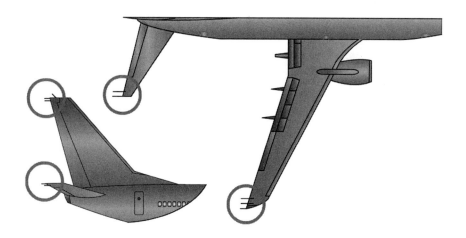

*Figure 8. Static Wick Locations*

the repeated striking of the electricity has fried the paint like some giant sewing needle working its way along the side of the plane. This is purely a cosmetic problem. Imagine the people sitting only a foot from those spots! Except for a huge flash and most definitely a loud "crack," they feel nothing. Airliners are designed to take zaps from Mother Nature now and then.

# Cruise: "It beats the heck out of driving"

Once your jet levels off at cruise altitude, things are pretty quiet. Call button tones and tones accompanying seat belt signs, as well as informational or instructional announcements from the pilots or Flight Attendants are about all you will hear. Relax and imagine where you would be if you were driving.

On a jet you are moving along at seven to eight miles per minute. One hundred miles is a scant 15 minutes at cruise speed. And, you are going nearly direct to your destination with few deviations, unlike a road that wanders all over the place. Next time you plan a road trip, overlay the road on the map with a piece or yarn. Then straighten out the yarn and see how much farther you have to drive along that wiggly road. Think back to the settlers walking alongside their Prairie Schooner wagons two hundred years ago. On an average day, they made seven miles. And that was usually walking alongside the wagon because it was full of their possessions. You are moving that distance in only 60 seconds. Even if you were in your car on the ground, it would take six to seven minutes to cover what you just flew in one minute. And that assumes the car was 60 miles per hour on a straight road without any turns.

In the winter, jet stream winds blow from the west at 100 mph or more. These winds are concentrated in a tight core, perhaps 100 miles in diameter and snake their way for thousands of miles across the country at high altitudes, usually above 20,000 feet (See Figure 9). If your flight path takes you through this area you can gain significant speed if you are lucky enough to be flying the same direction as the winds. If heading into them, your speed is reduced by the amount of the headwind. Most pilots will fly at lower altitudes in hopes of

*Figure 9. Jetstream Winds*

encountering fewer headwinds if fuel permits. Remember: Every knot of wind decreases/increases your flight time accordingly. A 70-knot tail wind means in one hour you will be approximately 70 nautical miles ahead of where you would have been without the wind (about ten minutes early). Conversely, the same wind in your face (headwind) will make you 10 minutes later after an hour in flight. Airlines account for differing winds as the seasons change and plan their schedules accordingly. Despite their best average wind forecasts, winds above normal occasionally make planes a few minutes late when flying into these winds (usually westbound flights). For planes going with the winds (usually eastbound), an early arrival can be expected.

This speed partly accounts for the safety statistics about flying. While flying is statistically safer than driving, much of this has to do with *exposure to risk*. In an hour flight from Phoenix to Los Angeles, you are nowhere near another plane except while on or near the ground.

In a car though, you'll spend at least seven hours on an interstate or freeway, often in busy traffic, with cars traveling at different speeds, driven by drivers with different levels of experience, sleep, and blood alcohol content. You'll spend that time guiding your vehicle between the white lines and watching the other cars to make sure they stay in their lane. You have to remain ever watchful for junk in the road, animals, and speed traps. All the while, navigating along changing roadways, sometimes in rain or blazing heat. These are but a few of the reasons flying beats the heck out of driving.

## Technical Stuff:

*Aircraft are separated by ATC which maintains a "bubble" of clear airspace around an aircraft (See Figure 10). Minimum vertical separation is 1,000 feet at altitudes below 29,000 feet with 2,000 feet vertical separation required above 29,000 feet. Soon, vertical separation will be reduced to 1,000 feet at all altitudes in an attempt to reduce en route delays, which helps airlines stay on time. Horizontal separation is usually in excess of two miles except in the airport traffic pattern. Near the airport if the weather is good enough for visual operations, pilots are warned of other approaching or nearby aircraft. Once the pilots see each other and acknowledge to ATC that they have each other in sight, they will often be released from instrument flight rules and allowed to operate their aircraft inside the ATC safety separation bubble. This "visual approach" is what keeps traffic moving into airports smoothly and efficiently and explains why you frequently see other airliners very close as they land on or depart adjacent parallel runways. Visual approach procedures allow the movement of a large number of planes very quickly. When visual conditions deteriorate to a point where pilots can no longer see other aircraft and the runway they are about to land on, ATC reverts to instrument procedures. That requires the increased separation bubble, which means more distance between aircraft landing and taking off. This creates delays over time as the rate of arrivals and departures declines. This may be a*

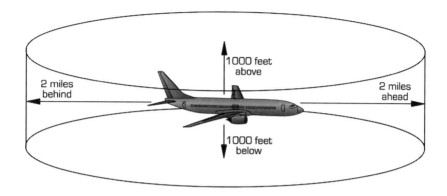

*Figure 10. ATC Bubble*

> short inconvenience early in the day, but by late after-
> noon to early evening, may mean delays of an hour or
> more for arriving aircraft.

## The View Outside

If you were lucky enough to grab a window seat, there's a whole world to watch outside. If you don't like what you see, wait ten minutes and the scenery will change.

Early in the morning or late in the evening when the sun is at a low angle, you may see the reflection of a mile or two of reflective highway signs lit by the sun. A car dealership or shopping center parking lot may glow red from the reflectors on the tail lights of the parked cars.

In the Plains states like Oklahoma, you'll notice hundreds, if not thousands, of tiny ponds reflecting on the ground. One of our pilots, also a cattleman, told me these small ponds were formed as buffalo wallows. Hundreds of years ago when the buffalo roamed the plains in vast numbers, they would roll in mud formed in small depressions after summer rains. Each buffalo would carry off upwards of 100 pounds of caked mud in their fur that was later shaken off as they walked across the prairie. One by one they acted like earthmovers, increasing the size of these wallows until now, many appear to be small shallow lakes from the air. The explanation sounds crazy at first, but makes sense after you think about it.

Over clouds, you may see a corona of bright pink reflected off the plane into the clouds. In combat, placing this "sun spot" over enemy planes meant you were safely hidden by the sun and the enemy pilots couldn't see you.

On the ground below, you can barely make out interstates or the vehicles on them during the day. At night the headlights are clearly visible from six miles up. Farms offer a carpet of green, or brown, depending on the season. Many people ask about the giant "green circles" or "Pac-Men" on the ground. These are farms that are watered by "Wonder Wheel" irrigation systems that have a well or piped water source at the center and utilize a long pipe, up to a quarter-mile long that rotates on wheels around the water source. The result is the circular growth pattern of the crops. Sometimes they only water a part of the circle leaving the "Pac Man" shape evident from the sky.

Geological features abound. The crusty edges of dry lakes clearly show where ancient lakeshores used to lie. Mountains out West look like upturned Neapolitan ice cream, with layers of sedimentary rock thrust upward, and clearly visible from the air. Nowhere else is the desert color so apparent than from the sky. Fields of wild flowers cast a colorful hue to the ground in certain areas like the northwest edge of the Mojave Desert when the poppies are in bloom.

Back East, as the trees turn orange and golden, they stand out like gaily-decorated generals, often in a sea of fellow evergreen troops. Boat wakes stretch out for miles on the Chesapeake on a calm day. Snow changes the texture as well as the color of the earth making things look decidedly otherworldly and often bitterly cold during winter.

Hopefully, your pilots will point out some of the more prominent features to you. Pilots occasionally get busy with weather concerns or other business. I try as a minimum to point out some prominent features, and give an update on position and arrival time at least each hour during the flight. The exceptions are on early morning or late night flights, where most passengers prefer to remain asleep, or on flights where cloud cover obscures the ground.

Passengers often wonder why the cabin is so cold on long flights. This depends on several factors. While it may be 65 degrees below zero outside the plane at 37,000 feet, each passenger is actually putting off heat inside the cabin. Multiplied times the number of passengers, this heat adds up. With a fairly full plane the heating system can add enough heat to keep everyone comfortably warm. The problem arises when the plane has been flying for more than an hour with less than a full passenger load and the cold outside finally starts to extract heat from the cabin. Heat rises and the heating sensors are near the ceiling. While the heating system is keeping the thermostat nicely warm up in the ceiling, four or five feet below seated in your seat, you are getting cold. Turning up the heat to warm the lower cabin floor makes it really toasty near the ceiling along the aisle.

The Flight Attendants are the real thermostats, as they inevitably call the pilots who control the heat to tell them they are freezing or burning up. Remember: The Flight Attendants are walking upwards of one to two miles on a long flight so their body temperatures are higher. **General rule:** if you are cold-natured, sit near the front of the plane because that section generally stays the warmest. The back of a near-empty plane can feel quite arctic-like.

# Descent

Your first clue that you are heading downhill is the sound of the engines slowly throbbing back to idle. Believe it or not, big jetliners actually glide incredibly well and they need no thrust to glide down to lower altitudes. Obviously, shutting the motors off is impractical and unwise, but without them a 737 at 41,000 feet could glide almost 80 miles to a sea level airport. In one case in the 1980s, a Boeing 767 actually did glide to a runway and a safe landing. This was an emergency event though and definitely not routine.

During the descent, ATC may request the pilots expedite their descent to a lower altitude, often for crossing traffic ahead. A tool they can use to do this is the "speed brakes", which are part of the spoiler array on the top of the wing (See Figure 11). These "boards," as pilots call them, pop up, destroying the lift across that small portion of the wing. This causes the rest of the wing to work harder to hold the plane up, and that results in higher drag, like a little parachute tied to the back of the plane which, in turn, helps the plane get down faster. The "boards" produce a characteristic rumble which vibrates the plane the more they are extended. Most of the vibration actually is disturbed airflow striking the tail of the plane. Yet another good reason to have a window seat: You can see the "boards" pop up on the wing. If you watch during landing, as soon as a wheel touches down the whole spoiler array pops up. This kills any lift produced by the wing and places more weight on the wheels to aid in braking.

In certain situations, the landing gear can be extended to provide more drag. Usually this is done at a slower speed for the comfort of passengers. But, on occasion and for a variety of reasons, the pilots may extend the gear to help expedite the aircraft's descent. This is characterized by the usual "CLUNK" as the main landing gear are unlocked and actually free-fall into the down position. At higher speeds the "wwWHOOSHHH" sound of the gear extending in the slipstream (the air whipping by the outside of the airplane) is a little bit higher than a normal on-speed deployment. Rest assured, this relatively unusual configuration is reserved for special cases. The extra noise and vibration is air drag doing its work to slow the plane down and/or help the plane descend faster. Amazingly, a maximum rate descent without the gear extended can produce vertical velocities of 5,000-6,000 feet per minute—sixty miles per hour. This results in a faster speed across the ground, which might make landing impossible if there is not enough distance between the plane and the runway to slow down. Extending the landing gear and flaps lets you descend at a steeper angle without getting that high speed across the ground. Sometimes for other traffic or other reasons, the plane gets held up higher than normal. The drag produced by the gear and flaps is what helps get the plane down to a low altitude with room enough to slow down in time to land. A car uses brakes to slow wheels in contact with

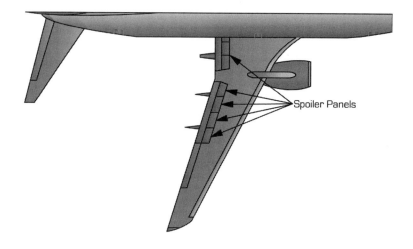

*Figure 11. Speedbrakes (Spoilers)*

the road. Inflight, a plane is only in contact with the air and drag is the only way (short of flying uphill) that a plane can slow down quickly or, more importantly, descend more steeply without building up speed.

## Landing

As the plane descends to the airport, the Air Traffic Controllers will guide it into the traffic flow with other aircraft. Many times you will feel the plane level off and the engines come in with power to keep the airspeed constant. Sometimes a pilot will just be leveling off at one speed when the controller directs him to slow further. The engines that were just speeding up may fall quiet again as the pilot adjusts his speed. Once near the desired airspeed, the power will come back in and stabilize.

Sometimes the pilots will be asked to slow to a speed that requires they extend some flaps. Flaps are what allow planes to fly slow enough to land and take-off comfortably on shorter runways (See Figure 12). You'll hear the flap motor running the trailing edge flaps out to the desired setting, one of many positions between "up" and "full down." The closer the plane gets to the runway the more times you'll hear this motor running. Normally, after the first or second "whir" from the flap motor, you'll hear the gear extend. Soon after the gear is extended, the flaps will be run down to their final landing position.

Once the flaps are down, the plane will slow quickly, and the pilot will bring the power in at a fairly high power setting to offset the enormous drag produced by the flaps. As the plane gets closer and closer to the ground, Mother Nature will conspire to speed the plane up or down, and the pilot will constantly be adjusting the power during the approach. In the summer this is most notable as the thermals bump the plane around. In the winter, once set, the pilot seldom has to adjust the power.

Seconds prior to touchdown, the pilot will reduce the power to idle, and the plane will settle down for a feather smooth landing. At least that is *the plan*.

> *Secret Pilot Stuff: On rainy days, you usually get really smooth landings as the water on the runway allows the tires to slide a bit and smoothly spin up at touchdown. On dry runways, the energy necessary to almost instantly spin up 500 pounds of wheels and tires to 100 plus miles per hour often results in a jolt to the plane right as it touches down, marring what would have otherwise been a smooth touchdown.*

People ask me if landing a jetliner is hard. After doing it nearly 10,000 times, I tell them that under certain weather conditions, landings can be "sporty," but most of the time, flying to touchdown is fairly mundane. I liken the challenge to parallel parking a car: With experience the task becomes fairly easy. But occasionally, and often without notice, you bump the curb. This often happens when you begin to think about what you're doing rather than just performing the task. Every pilot aims for the "greaser," but smooth landings occasionally elude even the best of pilots. How smoothly you touch down a 60-ton vehicle floating through the air at 150 mph is less important than getting the plane safely on the runway in the landing zone and stopped within the remaining runway.

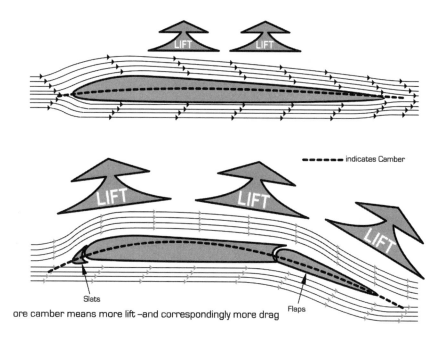

*Figure 12. Flaps and Slats*

On short runways, landing within the prescribed landing zone is absolutely critical. For example, Burbank Airport in California uses runway 08 as its prime runway, (08 being your compass heading as you fly down the runway or 080 degrees) which is 6,032 feet long. To distinguish the two ends of the runway, we call the end a plane flies over on approach the "approach" end. The other end is called the "departure" end. The approach end of the runway at Burbank has a blast fence to protect a perimeter road from jet and prop wind blasts. This fence is ten feet high and positioned right at the start of the runway. Only 6,032 feet later, sits another blast fence behind which sits another perimeter street with routine auto traffic zipping by. Figuring that the jet is flying across that first fence and clears it by a safe margin, the earliest safe location to touch down is about 1,200 to 1,500 feet down the runway leaving about 4,500 feet to get the aircraft stopped. That's all the room there is. You get one shot at landing at a runway of this type and, if your approach is not right, you have to quickly execute a "go-around" and fly another approach. A pilot floating a landing in search of a smooth touchdown is wasting critical pavement on which to stop the hurtling machine. I always check my ego in situations like this and go for the safe "in the landing zone" approach. I will save the floater/greaser approaches for runways nearly twice as long.

Is flying into short runways safe? Certainly, for highly experienced airline crews and other aviators with experience, it is done day-in and day-out in all kinds of weather. The experience and training of the crews is what makes this operation safe. This is another reason why they say pilots are compensated not so much for what they do, as for what they know. An old saying is, "A truly excellent pilot uses his good judgment to avoid situations where he has to use his superior flying skills."

Right after touchdown, the pilot will deploy the thrust reversers attached to the engine and the engines will "spool up" to near take-off power as diverted air slows the plane down. The engines do not actually "reverse." The airflow out the back of the engine gets diverted slightly forward and that helps slow the plane to a point where brakes are applied. Once slowed to taxi speed, the plane exits the runway and the flaps, spoilers, and thrust reversers are stowed. Motor "whines," "bumps," "clunks," and "howls" abound for a few seconds.

Occasionally when flying the older model 737 I'll get a report from a passenger that, upon landing, the engines fell apart. Some planes have reversers that are comprised of large clamshell doors that swing around to divert the air. This gives the appearance that big pieces of the engine are flailing around. I always ask the folks, "Right after the plane slowed down, did the pieces go back to where they originally were?" The answer, thus far, has always been, "Yes."

That's a basic flight, in a nutshell. I would like to touch on the landing phase in more detail because this phase of flight seems to cause the most concern to passengers and crew seated in the cabin.

# Landing: "Get this thing on the ground! And me outta here!"

Landings look a heck of a lot less scary from the front seat. In fact, they look the least scary to me when I am the one doing the landing. That's not a reflection on my partner who is quite capable of doing a fine job, but simply reflects the fact that PEOPLE LIKE TO BE IN CONTROL. This is why pilots make crummy passengers seated back in the cabin. They know what should be going on up front, but they aren't there to witness the activity for themselves. You folks in the back are totally "in the dark," and to many of you sitting up front in the cockpit wouldn't help much. Let me shed some light on "the landing phase."

Simply put, landing is the act of flying into the ground under very tightly controlled circumstances. Passengers give me nervous looks when I tell them this. In accordance with that universal truth of nature, "What goes up must come down," eventually every plane has to land. This is plain common sense. What most passengers don't realize is that when I am flying their plane down to touchdown, I am trying to land the *tires*, some twenty feet below and fifty feet behind me. If every pilot could get his or her wish, each would love to fly the plane to ½ inch of height between the main wheels and the runway. As the plane settled to the runway, this gradual settling would smoothly spin up the tires and provide the "greaser" landing all pilots strive for. If you get the tires on the ground smoothly, a smooth landing is pretty much assured. What happens to upset this effort?

About ten miles out from touchdown, the plane is about 3,000 feet above the runway. At that altitude the air is usually smooth. As the plane gets lower to the ground the ride gets a little bumpier as winds on the surface cause turbulence as they flow over buildings and other terrain features.

If Mother Nature bumps the plane to the left, the pilot makes a correction back to the right and then levels the wings again. The pilot has the plane lined up perfectly with the runway and is trying to hold that runway alignment while atmospheric conditions try to push the plane off course. One nervous flier told me she felt like the plane was, "trying to flip upside down," which is not the case. The plane is quite stable but keeps getting bumped off course slightly and the pilot is working harder and harder to keep the aircraft "in the slot"—a term we use to define a reasonable approach corridor. The plane has to be aligned with the runway horizontally and on a descent path (known as the "glide path") that is acceptable, all the while keeping the airspeed under control as the plane's descent rate changes due to turbulence. If you watch closely, the plane's movements will get faster and more precise as the plane gets closer and closer to touchdown. This description may sound alarming, but is simply the most fun the pilot will have in the course of the entire flight. Honest.

This is where sitting by the window really helps. You can look out and see how much the airplane is moving around in relation to the ground. With an aisle seat, the movements appear exaggerated and much more pronounced than they really are. This often leads to airsickness and is another reason I sit by the window. (See Chapter 9, "Aerospace Physiology," for why a window may help if you suffer from motion sickness.)

As the plane crosses the threshold of the runway, it may be buffeted slightly by thermals or turbulence thrown up by the wind's interaction to ground structures: trees, hangars, hills, cliffs, etc. The pilot has to correct for each of these intrusions. Occasionally, just prior to touchdown, the ride smoothes out, as if by magic. On a day when there are lots of thermals, especially in the summer, things can be downright uncomfortable at low altitudes. This isn't a problem for the pilots in terms of being able to control the plane, but makes getting that smooth landing a lot more challenging. Pilots call those conditions "sporty."

Once the pilot greases on the smoothest landing humanly possible, the thrust reversers are deployed. After the plane begins to slow, the pilot smoothly applies the brakes to slow the plane as the thrust reversers are stowed. If the First Officer has performed the landing, you might feel a little surge in the braking as the Captain comes on the brakes and takes control of the plane while the First Officer gets off his brakes in preparation to exit the runway. In most medium sized planes, the Captain does the taxiing, as the steering wheel for the nose wheel steering control is located on his side.

One note on aircraft brakes: They are *very* good at stopping the plane. Passengers rarely get to see the brakes at full application. Occasionally, the brakes will lurch on wet or bumpy runways as the anti-skid system momentarily releases pressure to the brakes when the tires begin to skid on the pavement. This is like the Anti-Skid Braking System (ABS) system in your car, and makes sure-footed braking possible in all kinds of weather.

That sums up the typical flight. Now that you know all these are normal sounds and feelings, when other less informed passengers look at your face to see if you are concerned, they'll see the look of confidence that comes with knowing everything is ho-hum normal. ("Yeah, *right!*") Believe me, they will.

Now to offer some insight as to how we make the impossible, *routine.*

*While changing planes at Atlanta's Hartsfield Airport, a couple found themselves coping with long distances between gates. Gratefully they headed towards a moving sidewalk. As the couple were about to step onto it, a grizzled gent in a cowboy hat and boots approached. Wearily shifting the two bulky bags he was toting, he asked, "Can you tell me if this sidewalk goes to Houston?"*

# Four:

# The Name of the Game

## Getting from A to B

**Sitting** inside the terminal or onboard an aircraft, especially in bad weather with delays or cancellations, one's mind naturally wanders to what brought us to this seemingly incomprehensible transportation system. How did flying become this complicated? Can the system possibly be as confusing as it appears from the passenger's perspective?

In that you will ultimately trust your life to this system as you fly within it on a commercial airliner, a look at how we actually go about preparing for a flight might help you better understand how the system works.

For example, let's look at a flight to Chicago. How do we go about planning the flight regarding issues such as, how much fuel to take; what to do about weather at our destination or en route; and what our options are if the weather takes a change for the worse?

Fuel is the most critical resource you can have inflight. Fuel literally *is* time. Having a little extra can mean the difference between diverting to an alternate, or being able to hold and wait for the weather to pass. Why not just fill up the plane's gas tanks? First, that might lead to people being left at the gate because the plane can only carry so much weight, given certain climatic conditions and available runway length. Second, it is very expensive to haul extra tons of fuel around, and the cost has to be outweighed by certain need. In some cases, one out of every three pounds of extra fuel carried is burned just to move the other two. We'll say for this example that the weather in Chicago is pretty close to the minimums we need to get in, and so we have Milwaukee listed as a good weather alternate, only 30 minutes away. How do we figure the fuel for this example?

The fueler knows how much fuel to load into the jet because the airline company Dispatchers issue what is known as a Flight Release. The Flight Release details the route of the flight, (often called the flight plan) detailing the number of miles flown by the jet on each leg of the flight to its destination. It displays the expected winds to be encountered by the flight as well as any turbulence warnings reported by other aircraft. Knowing the miles flown and the effect of winds on each segment, the flight-planning computer can generate a very accurate estimate of the time for each leg. Knowing this time and how much the plane burns on average each minute, the flight plan computer then determines the fuel burn at each point during the flight with a high degree of accuracy. In addition to the fuel required to fly to Chicago, additional fuel provisions are made for holding patterns or possible diversions to alternate airports, due to weather at the destination airport (See Figure 13).

If there is a chance the plane might not be able to land at the intended destination due to weather, an alternate airport with better weather is chosen as a backup alternate. Fuel is provided to allow the plane to fly to the destination, try an approach, and if necessary, fly to the designated alternate airport and land, still with 45 minutes of fuel on board. If the weather at the alternate airport is marginal, a second alternate will be specified farther away in better weather in the event the weather at the first alternate deteriorates. Additional fuel may be provided for holding if there is enough weight capacity available on the plane. This amount of fuel is uploaded into the aircraft by the fueler.

*"Ray, why are you telling us all this complicated stuff about weather, alternates, and fuel planning? What is the point?"*

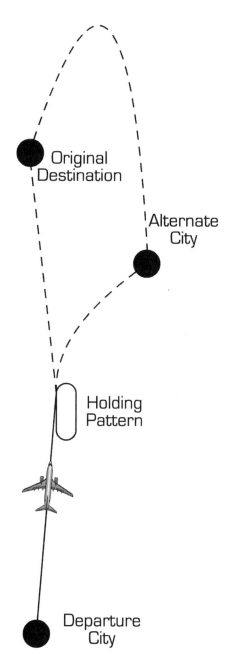

*Figure 13. Flight Planning*

The point is, way back in the infancy of aviation, somebody with an airplane offered to fly someone from A to B. With no weather system with which to check the destination weather, no en route navigation aids, no approach aids, and no concept of what to do if the destination weather worsened, they took off. Those who survived the flights swore there had to be a better way. This whole system of flight planning and aviation aids was created over many years, based partly on disaster, and a good part on the experience of seasoned aviators to make this business a whole lot safer. Modern aviation safety is based on common sense borne of experience.

An airliner has a large lifting capacity and can either carry full fuel tanks or a full load of passengers and bags, but usually not both, especially in the summer. On the ground, hot air is thin air and engines don't put out full thrust in thin air. Less thrust means less weight can be carried on the plane. Jet fuel weighs about eight pounds per gallon. Because baggage and people are weighed in pounds, we choose to measure gas in pounds for simplicity. If we fill the fuel tanks we may have to leave passengers behind, due to performance limitations of the aircraft. How much fuel needs to be loaded on the plane is carefully determined by coordination of the Flight Dispatcher, Pilot, and Operations Agent. The Ops Agent is the person actually conducting the boarding process, and at my airline, this person does the all-important take-off weight and balance computations. As in our example to Chicago, weather is a factor. Frequently, weather concerns and all the alternate planning considerations don't apply because the weather at our destination is good. In that case, we simply want to load the plane as efficiently as possible.

On occasion, we will take off knowing that we will have to stop short of our intended destination for fuel. This is rare, but often is the quickest and simplest way to accommodate a heavy travel season in the summer, especially out of high altitude airports. An example:

Once, in the middle of summer, due to an airplane substitution, I found myself flying an older 737 model with less performance capability than the newer model I was originally supposed to have flown. My next flight to St. Louis was right at the weight limit for the older plane, given the temperature and elevation of Salt Lake, my departure airport. The airline sold seats weeks prior to the flight based on a certain type of equipment normally scheduled for this route. Airline dispatch advised me that the flight was to go out nearly full, and we either had to leave passengers behind or stop in Kansas City for fuel, en route. Weight is weight, whether passengers or fuel, and the plane can only carry so much. Wanting to accommodate all the passengers, I agreed to the gas stop. As the Captain, the decision was up to me. There happened to be an ATC flow program (read: delays—explanation to follow) into St. Louis that day with half-hour delays. Kansas City is only about a half an hour away from St. Louis by air. Because Kansas City was not affected by the flow delay, we departed immediately. After a 15-minute fuel stop in Kansas City, we were advised there was no delay from Kansas City to St. Louis because by now the flow program had been terminated. Again we took off without a delay. We actually arrived in St. Louis *earlier* that day by stopping along the way instead of going non-stop. Weird, but true.

To understand these aircraft performance limitations, which determine how many people and how much fuel we can carry to Chicago, a review of take-off planning is necessary. My aim is not to teach you how to do performance computations but to take comfort in knowing, as a passenger, that if the worst thing imaginable happens (an engine fails right as the aircraft lifts off) this extremely remote, yet critical possibility has already been planned for in great detail.

## Planning for the Worst: Engine Failure on Take-off

Pilots generally agree that an aircraft is hardest to fly when heavyweight. The heaviest a jetliner will be throughout an entire flight is the weight of the aircraft at take-off. As the jetliner begins the take-off roll, the engines must accelerate not only the structure of the plane and weight of the passengers and baggage, but all the fuel the jet will need throughout the flight. With one engine inoperative, the performance needed to maintain even level flight demands incredible power from the remaining engine(s), and this unbalanced thrust condition makes the plane a challenge for pilots. The worst possible time for an engine failure to occur is right after we have made the decision on the runway to fly. Often times, there is not enough runway left at this point to stop, so we *must* go airborne. The decision to fly or stop is not one to be made lightly and relies on complex computations involving the weight of the aircraft, atmospheric conditions and runway length available for takeoff. This "GO/NO GO speed" is determined before the aircraft ever takes the runway. With the ground near and obstacles like trees, buildings, and towers abundant, the aircraft must be able to safely climb above these obstacles and land on a suitable runway either at the departure airport or another airport nearby. Pilots practice this maneuver in a simulator until they get the procedure down cold. Engine-out maneuvering during training is one of the most demanding and exacting tasks the new pilot will learn and it is practiced throughout a pilot's career.

> *"Captain Stark, you're not going to launch into more complicated wah-wah about planning, are you?"*

This explanation is fairly straightforward and explains why sometimes passengers are left at the gate as well as being crucial to the safety of those aboard. Attempt a take-off at a weight heavier than the remaining engine(s) can handle, and you will be unable to fly. Stick with me on this one.

By FAA regulation, all commercial jet aircraft (excluding most older propeller driven commuter planes) must be able to accelerate to take-off speed and either:

A: **liftoff** from the runway after losing an engine right at rotation (the point where the nose rotates up off the ground just prior to liftoff), climb to a safe altitude (usually 1,000 feet above the airport), and remain clear of obstacles, *OR*

B: abort the take-off and **stop** in the runway remaining (See Figure 14).

Clearly, if the runway is a zillion miles long, the only question is whether the plane is capable of flying away from the ground to 1,000

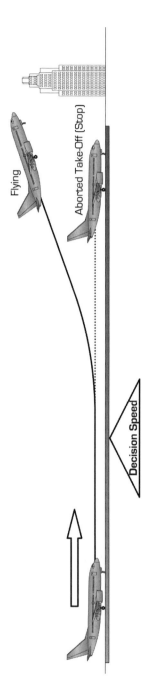

*Figure 14. Take-off/Abort*

feet (clear of trees and other obstacles) with one engine out. There is plenty of runway to stop should the take-off be aborted. However, should the runway be shorter, now abort (stopping) capability must be considered and these limitations also determine how much the plane can weigh.

The engines are only powerful enough to accelerate a given weight to take-off speed in the runway distance available. Similarly, the brakes are only able to stop the plane in the runway remaining from a finite speed should the need arise. This balance of opposing restrictions is critical and explains why, should the worst possible event occur (engine failure right at rotation), the aircraft will be able to climb clear of obstacles and return to land. This single problem also accounts for why the engines and brakes in newer jets are so much more powerful than older jets. Again, the concerns are safety, first and foremost.

### *"Okay, we're not too heavy to fly. What happens next?"*

Once the determination is made that our plane is within allowable weights, we are legal to depart. But we need clearance to actually fly our plane into controlled airspace. This is granted by the FAA in the form of an ATC clearance. Airliners operate in what is known as controlled airspace (see Figure 15), which is usually the area 20 miles around a major airport from the ground to 18,000 feet and all altitudes above 18,000 feet. The area is called controlled airspace because ATC is in contact with all aircraft in that airspace. ATC ensures all planes maintain a safe distance from one another through controller-directed clearances to climb, descend, or turn. Every move is under the watchful eye of Air Traffic Controllers and ATC computers looking for potential conflicts, and all aircraft closely follow ATC instructions. This maintains the "safety bubble" between aircraft that we discussed in the last chapter.

Pilots fly the airplane and navigate as they go along. Their job is keeping the plane operating within parameters, out of danger, and on course. As we discussed earlier, Air Traffic Controllers (ATC) are primarily charged with keeping airplanes flying blind in the weather,

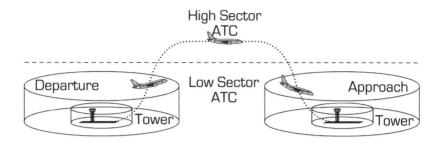

*Figure 15. ATC Sectors*

separated from one another as they climb, cruise, and descend to their destinations. A common misconception is that pilots can see other aircraft on their radarscopes: This is not really true. Modern aircraft radar is used primarily to identify weather ahead of the aircraft. To maximize efficiency, controller's use cleverly designed departure and arrival procedures to keep the aircraft clear of any high terrain, as well as other aircraft while in congested areas as they either climb on departure or descend to land. These serve to keep traffic moving, but separated, like onramps and offramps near a busy freeway interchange. When aircraft are in the lower altitudes, and if meteorological conditions allow good enough visibility, pilots may be allowed to fly "visually." This means the pilots can see well enough to see the airport and any aircraft that may pose a threat. The pilots may then be cleared to operate their aircraft to remain clear of other aircraft traffic and ground terrain features based on visual clues. Above 18,000 feet, everything is handled like it was "pea-soup" fog. Both pilots and Air Traffic Controllers rely on ATC ground based radar to keep aircraft separated. You can see why a radar outage really "hammers" the system and delays departures and arrivals.

In situations where a plane enters controlled airspace without permission, this intruding aircraft is sighted on ATC radar or visually by an aircraft under ATC control, and other nearby aircraft are warned and, if necessary, directed away from the offending aircraft. Smaller general aviation planes may be cleared to operate in this airspace if they are equipped with proper identification equipment (those transponders we talked about earlier), but generally remain clear of controlled airspace. The whole purpose of controlled airspace is to keep planes separated. This is how planes can fly blind in weather. ATC radar tracks their every move keeping them separated. TCAS (the collision avoidance system) allows other aircraft under ATC control to be displayed in the cockpit but this is primarily for close-quarter avoidance. TCAS does not take the place of an Air Traffic Controller who sees the "big picture." Pilots rely on ATC to tell them where other planes are and to keep aircraft separated and moving smoothly throughout the ATC system.

Another important part of "controlled airspace" is keeping aircraft flying in the blind clear of terrain obstacles as they climb and descend at lower altitudes. Minimum Vectoring Altitudes (MVAs) or "floors" are altitudes, which represent the lowest safe altitude a plane may be flown under radar control without the ground in sight. MVA's are issued by ATC and monitored to ensure aircraft do no not venture too close to the ground.

To operate within controlled airspace, you must have permission or a "clearance" to proceed with your flight. The first step in obtaining ATC clearance for an airliner is initiated by an airline Dispatcher or pilot submitting a computerized flight plan into the ATC computer system. Upon request for clearance by the pilot, ATC then clears the flight by radio prior to the plane's departure. This written and verbally confirmed clearance assures that the pilots know the planned route the company has requested has been accepted by the ATC system, and everyone involved is playing from the same sheet of music. Sometimes, due to weather or traffic saturation, (ATC jargon for airborne traffic jams), ATC will issue the clearance with restrictions, reroutes, or even ground delays, like the example I used going to St. Louis. How does ATC determine who gets to wait on the ground and who gets to take-off?

Airplanes cannot stop dead in the air, and when there is a bottleneck somewhere, planes en route to that destination sometimes enter "holding." Holding is a way to put jets "on pause" momentarily, to allow the bottleneck ahead to clear up. Unfortunately for ATC, jets in holding gobble up huge chunks of airspace as they fly around in circles, and that further adds to the airborne congestion problem. So, the FAA folks have assigned the seemingly impossible task of managing the orderly flow of jets to Flow Control, in Washington D.C. These specialists will hold planes on the ground for a predetermined time, to allow the orderly flow of planes into a given city. Imagine how tough this must be considering planes bound for Los Angeles, for example, can come from close cities like Phoenix, only an hour away while others come from New York, a good five hours away. All these planes must take off so as to arrive in a nice orderly fashion, not all bunched together. Talk about headaches. (Flow Control was the culprit that threatened to delay my flight from Salt Lake to St. Louis that I described earlier. Flow times are often referred to as "slot times" or "void times.")

These flow delays may be weather related, perhaps airport closures earlier in the day with back-ups the rest of the day, or just routine rush hour traffic. Even after the plane takes off, ATC controllers may request aircraft adjust their speed up or down so as to preclude everyone from arriving at once. This is often why the plane arrives later than the pilots told you it would in their "Folks, we just leveled off and the seatbelt sign is off, we expect to arrive on time" announcement.

The plane may be delayed for other reasons too. If weather makes the chances of actually arriving at the destination less than realistic, the pilot may, in coordination with Dispatch and other agencies, decide to wait out the delay on the ground rather than risk diverting to another city. Remember, if loading allows, the pilot may order enough extra fuel for the flight to hold for a short period if necessary. If weight becomes a problem, extra holding gas may not be an option.

Again, let's say our flight to Chicago has a good flight plan with a just-in-case alternate of Milwaukee, where the weather is good. We depart for Chicago and as we get nearer the weather worsens. What to do? (I'm going to lift a secret veil here so pay close attention.)

# Flying Blind—The Instrument Environment

Most people know planes can fly in clouds. How they do so remains a mystery.

Pilots need a reference for where up is and where down is to maintain control of their aircraft in clouds. Flying is impossible without visual cues, either real or artificial. Many inexperienced pilots have tried to rely on seat-of-the-pants feelings in a situation where visual orientation is lost, usually with catastrophic results. JFK Jr's accident was an example of this phenomenon that made headlines. The ability to safely fly in situations where routine visual information is not available, as is the case inside clouds or at night, takes a pilot trained in instrument procedures. Airline pilots have practiced their skills for years. Much of that training was flying aircraft, or simulators, in an instrument environment using the dash mounted flight instruments as the sole means of position orientation. The primary instrument pilots rely on is the artificial horizon, which the pilot must trust implicitly regardless of any feelings his or her balance system may be offering. This is a skill honed over many, many hours of experience and is done routinely every time they fly. But just keeping the "shiny side up" won't navigate the plane across the country and land the plane for you.

En route navigation is done either by ground based radio beacons, or navigation aids called "navaids." These navaids transmit an invisible compass rose of 360 radials, like a pie viewed from the sky cut into 360 slices, telling the pilot where he is directionally in relation to the navaid (see Figure 16). Most navaids also transmit a distance indication from the navigation aid facility telling the pilot how far away the aircraft is from the navaid in miles. Knowing which direction and how far away this reference point is tells the pilot his location and in which direction to fly. Newer planes navigate by satellites which involves using time delays from signals sent out by several satellites to triangulate very precise positions. This system is known as Global Positioning Satellites or GPS (See Figure 18). GPS gives position information, including altitude, to within feet where the

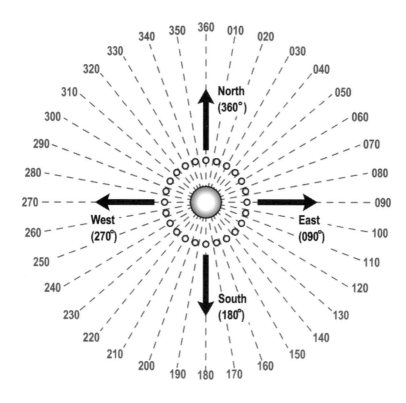

*Figure 16. VOR illustration showing radials in 10 degree increments.*

older ground base navaids sometimes are off by a couple of miles. This GPS system is the same one that tells modern auto navigation systems where the car is. (Paid for by your Department of Defense tax dollars.)

Pilots fly "roads in the sky" defined by navaids on the ground or points created in space by GPS satellites (See Figure 17). These jet routes serve to make order out of the chaos that would surely result if everybody went directly on their way. Ever been in a shopping center parking lot when people start driving across rows rather than down the rows? Imagine the sky filled up with thousands of planes going hundreds of miles per hour in different directions, and you get a feel for the magnitude of the problem, and the need for order.

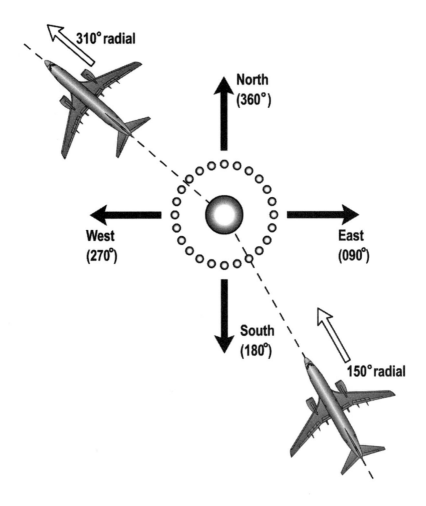

*Figure 17. VOR Synoptic*

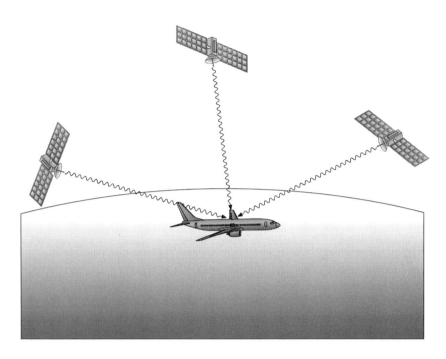

*Figure 18. Global Positioning System (GPS)*

Sometimes a pilot may get clearance to proceed directly to points further along the route if other planes don't pose a conflict. This is how we "take shortcuts" and sometimes get to our destinations early. We call this maneuver "cutting the corner." A large part of the airspace in this country is used for military training. We plan to go around these areas but, if the airspace is not in use, we may be allowed to cut that corner and fly a more direct route through the inactive military airspace to our destination. That gets us most of the way, but we still have to land.

Let's say our Chicago flight has flown all the way to the border of Illinois. There were a few thunderstorms and rain showers en route but we simply flew around the worst weather while up at cruising altitude. Now as we get closer to our destination, and lower to the ground, there is a line of rain showers building into thunderstorms that will be crossing the airport about the time we arrive. Our pilots know this by checking the latest airport weather broadcast, and by *painting* the weather on their weather radar as they get closer to the airport. Painting refers to the aircraft radar, which actually "paints" weather ahead in a bath of microwave energy. Denser material like rain or ice causes the radiation to reflect back to the aircraft where it is displayed on the radar screen. With no safety issues to indicate that they ought to go elsewhere, the pilots agree to begin the approach into Chicago. The clouds in the area are close to the ground and an instrument approach will be necessary to get the plane positioned near the approach end of the runway in order for the pilots to see the runway and land.

## Flying To The Ground—Blind

> *Instrument Approach: A landing, whereby the pilots maneuver the plane solely based on their instruments, descending to a point near the end of the runway, where they will either see the runway and land, or continue flying, remaining on instruments, climbing clear of obstacles (the go-around).*

Other specialized types of navaids are used for landing (see Figure 19). These are generally much more precise than en route navaids and are designed to safely allow the plane to fly to a point at the beginning of the runway and to land (if the pilots can see the runway), or go-around (if they can't see it). This concept is critical to understanding instrument flight. Note that you plan to *either* land *or* go-around depending on whether or not the pilot sees the runway. Another way of thinking: An approach to a planned go-around is interrupted by seeing the runway and landing. Don't be alarmed if the pilot starts a go-around in the middle of the approach. Pilots are prepared to go-around *before* they start the approach. They brief out loud a review of the approach they will fly and part of that briefing includes where to fly if they can't see the runway. The go-around is a normal, well practiced and planned maneuver all spelled out on the approach chart. (See Figure 20).

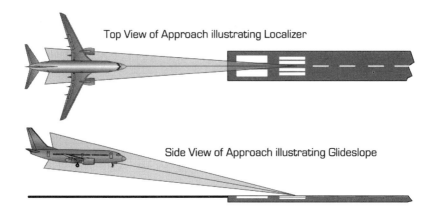

*Figure 19. Instrument Landing System (ILS)*

Think for a moment about the options a pilot has at the point on the approach where the runway should come into view, but does not. Should the pilot continue descending into the weather, towards the ground with no visual clues? Absolutely not! A go-around is the only safe option. Remember, the whole purpose of an approach is to get the plane in a position near the runway where the pilot can take over visually. Even on planes that are certified to fly in near zero visibility, the pilot still has to be able to see the runway. Think of a go-around in kid terms: a go-around is like a do-over. Taking the aircraft around for another approach only costs a little bit of gas and time. Most people never experience one, but when they do, they are surprised because they were mentally prepared to land, and suddenly they find themselves taking off again. Go-arounds are *good* things.

On occasion, the go-around is begun way before the plane gets to the point where the pilot expects to see the runway. Suppose the plane in front of you blows a tire and stops on the runway you intend to land on? You guessed right, a go-around. Unless another runway is immediately available, the pilots have no choice. Go-arounds begun a mile or so away from the runway can be smooth and gentle, as there is

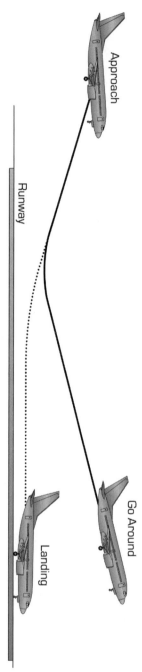

*Figure 20. Go Around*

plenty of time to change from landing to take-off mode. During low visibility when the plane is down to the lowest altitude and the runway has not been sighted by the "missed approach point," the pilot must quickly execute the maneuver. This rapid response ensures that the aircraft remains within a clear safety area clear of ground obstacles. These go-arounds are the most alarming to passengers because they happen abruptly but this is by design and is for your safety.

Before a pilot can begin an approach, the weather must be above "minimums." This term applies to the minimum FAA visibility requirements necessary to fly the approach. Usually, minimum visibility is about one half of a mile for most precision approaches. You need to be able to see at least a half-mile to be able to see the runway and land the plane. Should the weather fall below this "minimum," the pilots are not even allowed to begin the approach. Holding or diversion is the only option unless there is another approach to a different runway that is "above minimums" (i.e. you can see well enough to land). Having weather above minimums does not necessarily guarantee the pilots will be able to see the runway to land. Often cloud layers are ragged on their bottom sides and they randomly obscure the runway. Also, the visibility measured on the ground may be advertised at something above what the pilots see inflight. When the weather is right at minimums the pilot flying the aircraft will literally have about one second to decide whether to land—if the runway comes into view, or begin the missed approach and go around.

When the weather is right at minimums, the pilot may have to take a couple of tries at the approach in hopes of arriving at that point in space over the runway threshold precisely as the weather clears momentarily. When the pilot tells the passengers, "We are going to give it another shot," this is what is meant. (On the previous attempt, clouds obscured the runway and the pilot will fly another approach, hoping to see the runway and land.) Going around is staying safe when the runway isn't in sight. Take comfort in the blast of power from those big engines. They are getting you away from the ground and back to the safety of altitude.

Some aircraft have an "auto-land" feature that enables the plane to land itself with virtually no forward visibility at all. These systems are useful on occasion but extremely expensive to maintain.

A newer system called the Heads Up Display or HUD actually gives airlines more capabilities for much less upkeep cost, and many airlines have decided to install these devices (see Figure 21). Using the HUD, the pilot actually "hand flies" the plane while looking through the HUD, and is prepared to land the instant the runway appears. My company has decided, if you can't get there with a HUD, maybe it's best to wait the weather out. (HUD's—more of that taxpayer funded military technology making our lives easier. General Motors is even installing a version of the HUD on some new automobiles to display infrared images of obstacles or threats ahead.)

# Back to Our Chicago Flight— 100 Miles From Touchdown

The pilots have received word from the approach controllers that a tight band of very heavy rain is falling over the airport, and the visibility is below minimums for the approach to Chicago. The pilots elect to wait out the rain, which is expected to pass shortly and the flight enters a holding pattern. While holding, the pilot's further review the approach they are about to fly, and develop a game plan should the weather begin to worsen.

Ten minutes later, the approach controller advises the pilots that the Chicago airport tower controllers are reporting better visibility, but another strong line of rain showers is approaching quickly from the south. The pilots elect to begin the approach, hoping to beat the impending weather. Ever present in the pilot's mind, is any telltale sign that weather conditions are reaching a point where safety is compromised. The pilot has discussed this concern with his partner and they are prepared to instantly break off the approach and avoid the approaching weather.

The plane is cleared by ATC to begin the approach. As the pilots break out of the clouds and sight the runway, they also see a dust

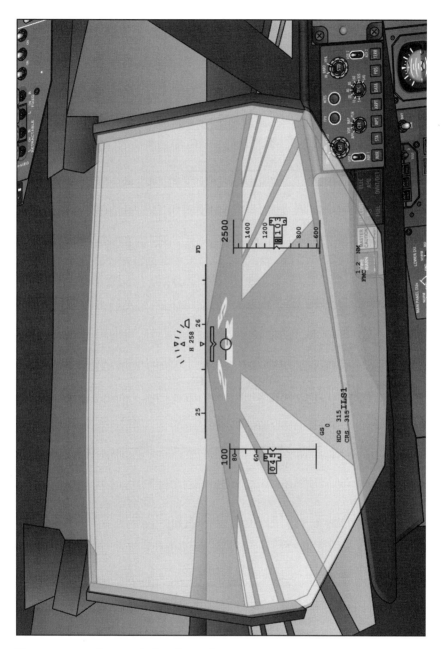

*Figure 21. Heads Up Display (HUD)*

cloud being blown in from the approaching weather. Wind speed instruments in the tower indicate fifty mile per hour winds are already blowing at the far end of the runway, though the winds at the approach end are relatively steady and within limits. The winds at altitude are making the ride pretty bumpy. The Captain makes the decision to escape the oncoming storm and the pilots announce their intentions to ATC. The First Officer requests an immediate right turn to avoid the weather and the flight is cleared to do so. Now what to do?

So far, the pilots have waited out the first band of weather, and then attempted an approach between moving weather systems. Rather than attempt a landing in worsening conditions, with no idea when the system will move completely through the airport area, the Captain elects to proceed to Milwaukee, his planned alternate. Thirty minutes later, the plane pulls into the gate in Milwaukee under scattered clouds.

Upon arrival, the Captain calls Mother, (company dispatch), and is advised that the weather has moved through the Chicago area. By taking a westerly approach, the flight can avoid most of the storm. The Captain signs a new release for the flight and then advises the passengers of the plan. The plane was refueled while the Captain was talking to dispatch and is now ready to fly to Chicago.

An hour and fifty minutes late, the flight pulls into Chicago, safe and sound.

This seemingly endless example is but a simplification of what goes on during an ordinary flight, and a peek into the key roles played by the pilots, air traffic controllers, airline dispatch, and weather personnel. They must all use good judgment in an ever-changing environment, and make alternative plans in case their original plans don't work.

As a pilot, my main job responsibility is decision-making. I must not allow my plane and passengers to be forced down one path. I must use my experience and training to constantly consider every other option available and avoid being "backed out on a limb." This increases my chances of success and survival. Decision making ability is the essence of the experienced aviator.

While aspects of this chapter may have seemed *dry* to the reader, what happens behind the scenes is critical to understanding how carefully a flight is planned and managed and how many things *we* worry over so that *you* shouldn't have to. In the next chapter we will look at more background reasoning and some of the preparation that gets you to your destination.

*On a cross-country flight a passenger tried a technique a friend had recommended for controlling fear. She asked the Flight Attendant for a magazine, some paper and a pencil, and proceeded to copy the words from each page of the magazine. It was tedious, but effectively distracting. Several articles later, the attendant approached her. "I admire your thrift," she said. "But please, just keep the magazine—compliments of the airline."*

# Five:

# Making Sure Things Go Right

## ALWAYS—Somebody Drive the Plane

**The** safety record of modern commercial aviation is, in no small part, due to the efforts of engineers who have refined the machines we fly in today. Years of experience in aircraft design has allowed them to not only make the "box" we fly in lighter, stronger, and much more reliable, but they have also refined other potential problem areas that, in the past, have led to accidents.

Past accidents have been caused, in part, by things as simple as which way a switch moved to the "off" position. The "man-machine" interface has been examined so intensely that all the systems in the plane are now either automated, with manual back-ups just in case, or they require little or no attention from the pilots. Systems that require pilot input during the flight are much more intuitive and simple. Today, the aircraft itself is found to be the primary cause in only 10 percent of all jet accidents.

This examination of how humans and machines work together has led engineers to further examine the human-to-human interaction of the crew. This review has become known as Crew Resource Management (CRM), and has been widely accepted by not only the civilian commercial community, but by the U.S. military as well. CRM is as essential to the safe operation of the aircraft as bolting the wings on securely or making sure there is enough fuel. All crewmembers must operate as part of a cooperative unit, each aware of the other's performance and contribution to the mission at hand. Each must be willing to speak up if anything does not "look" right. Without this cooperative approach to the highly technical job of flying, you may well have a superbly designed machine operated by one person, or, as in some sad instances in the past, no one.

Eastern Airlines suffered an accident some twenty-five years ago in the Florida Everglades that was found to stem from so simple a cause, that it reverberated through commercial aviation and changed the industry forever.

One evening, as an Eastern Jumbo Jet (L-1011) descended inbound to Miami, the pilots noticed that one of the light bulbs indicating the position of the landing gear was burned out. No big deal, with hundreds of light bulbs in the cockpit, this is a daily occurrence. The problem centered on the fact that the entire crew became so busy trying to troubleshoot a possible system problem, that was later realized to be a simple burned out light bulb, they all stopped paying attention to the task at hand: flying the plane.

The result was that nobody noticed the airplane had started a very slow descent. This descent continued unnoticed for thousands of feet. When the Ground Proximity Warning System (GPWS) alerted the crew they were facing imminent contact with the ground, they discounted the warning, thinking they were still at cruise altitude. When they finally realized the plane was about to touch down, it was too late. A perfectly good aircraft was allowed to fly itself into the Everglades for the want of a light bulb. Fortunately, many passengers survived.

In the accident investigation, investigators revealed that, simply put, nobody was flying the aircraft. No one was minding the store. Everyone on the flight deck allowed their attention to be drawn to the light bulb situation, with catastrophic results.

A consequence of this accident was a drastic re-think of how individual crews work together. Two major rules evolved to prevent a reoccurrence of this type accident. One cardinal common-sense rule that resulted was, ALWAYS, SOMEBODY FLY THE AIRCRAFT. In the past, this was left more to "pilot technique" than actually taught in training. Now, the first thing out of a Captain's mouth when something occurs is, "I've got the airplane," or, "You've got the airplane, I'm going into the checklist." This critical detail of making sure nobody forgets to fly the aircraft is drilled into pilots during training and largely due to this one accident.

Secondly, when the crew was notified by the system that is designed precisely to warn them they were about to hit the ground, they delayed their response in disbelief of the alarms authenticity. What harm would have come to the plane and crew if they had received a bogus terrain avoidance warning and instantly begun a climb at 15,000 feet? None whatsoever. By the time the plane had descended to 100 feet, the response time to evade the ground was very short. Today, pilots are expected to instantly respond to warnings such as the Ground Proximity Warning System (GPWS) and sort out whether the alarm is a real ground proximity event or bogus malfunction later. There is precious little time to analyze when the warning sounds.

## Dial-a-Disaster

A great way to put crews into the heat of battle without risk is by simulating the flight with flight simulators. Commercial pilots are required to visit training centers on a recurring basis. During these simulated flights, crews explore all kinds of emergency situations they might encounter in service. Emergencies and malfunctions are administered by a watchful instructor or evaluator who sits right behind the crew in the same cockpit. This simulator operator can select from hundreds of aircraft system malfunctions ranging from minor to catastrophic. For this reason, I call the simulator experience, "Dial-a-Disaster."

Every single problem a crew can encounter, from engine failure on take-off, to wind shear on landing, can be faithfully reproduced for the crew to experience. The simulators are aircraft cockpits mounted on large hydraulic legs, which give a limited "seat-of-the-pants" reality to the flight maneuver (see Figure 22). Incredibly complex video images are provided to simulate the view out the cockpit windows. For the many who have flown the excellent computer based home flight simulators available today, the real full-motion simulator is truly an astonishingly realistic ride. Many major theme parks like Disneyland and Universal Studios have thrill rides mounted on aircraft style simulator bases to give that motion experience. These are some of the most popular rides to date. As good as aircraft simulators are, their shortcomings actually serve to help in training pilots.

Pilots are a stubborn bunch. We are held to a high standard of performance both by ourselves and by the system in which we operate. The simulator is an opportunity to "load up" the crew with many complex tasks, testing their limits. To resolve the numerous problems before them, the pilots have to prioritize, integrate their solutions to, and resolve the system malfunctions according to detailed procedural checklists. The experience is *work*, plain and simple. Remember: There is still the task of flying the plane while troubleshooting the problem and accomplishing these checklists.

Further, simulators are great training aids, but they are not airplanes. When not on autopilot, they tend to wander off altitude or slowly enter uncommanded rolls, which require constant correction and attention from the pilot. Initially, this is supremely challenging for the pilot, but once a skill is mastered in the "box," as we call the simulator, it means that if the pilot were actually in the plane, his or her performance would be significantly better. The plane is a lot easier to fly than the "box." Imagine hopping on one foot while rubbing your stomach with one hand and playing a video game with the other hand, all the while talking to someone on the telephone while the person next to you asks you questions. Imagine that instruments measure your performance in every detail. Measurements of how high you jump, how far you move from a given point, and how smoothly you continue to rub your stomach. Also imagine that someone is watching your performance, grading you on how you respond to the questions coming from your partner. This analogy

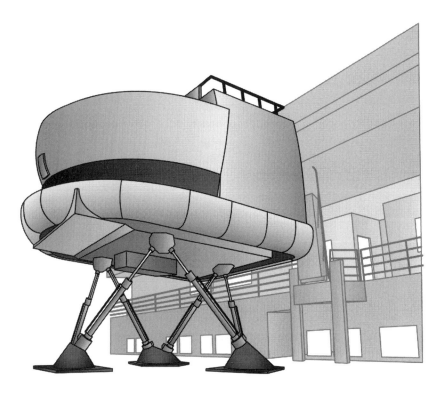

*Figure 22. Flight Simulator*

describes what flying a simulator can be like. Most people agree using a cell phone while driving a car is tough. Pilots become *very* good at performing several tasks at once. Multi-tasking is essential for survival.

## Technical Stuff:

> *Think I'm kidding about the jumping-on-one-foot-and-rubbing-your-stomach example? I mentioned engine failure at take-off earlier as a procedure we practice relentlessly. Here's an idea of just some of the items that go through the pilot's mind as the event occurs during take-off:*
>
> *—"Cleared for take-off, brakes released...*

79

*—Stand up the throttles to mid-power—let both engines accelerate....*

*—Throttles to Take-off Power setting....*

*—Engines stabilized at take-off power setting....*

*—Keep the aircraft on centerline....*

*—Double-check engine instruments....*

*—Centerline—crosswind picking up—keep off those pesky centerline "dots"....*

*—"Vee One" call by pilot not flying indicating we are committed to take-off....*

*—"BANG" (loud noise of engine failing accompanied by warning lights and alarm bell)....*

*—WE ARE GOING AIRBORNE—no aborts allowed after V1 callout....*

*—Must add much more rudder to keep aircraft on centerline as remaining engine tries to steer aircraft towards right and off of runway....*

*—"Rotate" call by pilot not flying (PNF) indicating the aircraft is at flying speed....*

*—Move control yoke aft SLOWLY and fly aircraft off runway in controlled manner using less rudder as speed increases, maintaining wings level and constant heading....*

*—"Gear UP!" command to pilot not flying to raise landing gear....*

*—Heading? Wandering off slightly due to too much rudder—let off a bit. Any rudder change requires a change in ailerons to keep wings level.*

*—PNF advises me he has silenced the Fire Warning fire bell—I am so busy I never noticed it ringing—Acknowledge pilot not flying punching off fire alarm bell and entering checklist once safely established on climbout....*

*—Too much rudder and the plane rolls precariously or wanders off course, too little and the result is the same....*

*—Airport tower calls to advise of fireball from right engine as we rotated for take-off—Instruct non flying pilot*

*to relay emergency status to tower while maintaining safe climb straight out or as necessary due to terrain limitations....*

*—Pitch? Too steep and the plane slows rapidly. Too shallow and the aircraft will not climb away from ground obstacles....*

*—Airspeed? Slow too much and the aircraft will become uncontrollable. Too much speed and we are wasting valuable time to get to emergency level off altitude and away from ground....*

*—Pitch?...adjust*

*—Airspeed?...adjust*

*—Heading?...adjust*

*—Any special departure procedures in the event of engine failure? Thankfully, not on this departure—just climb to 1,000 feet above the ground and clean up the aircraft (raise flaps and gear) and get in the checklist to resolve situation and shutdown the problem engine....*

*—PNF announces which checklist he is about to enter and asks for my concurrence—Must quickly evaluate the engine indications: No rotation on engine number two, Number two engine fire warning is illuminated... Looks like a bona fide engine fire. Instruct PNF to enter the Engine Fire checklist....*

*—Pitch?...adjust*

*—Airspeed?...adjust*

*—Heading?...adjust*

*—Crank in rudder trim to help with 80-90lbs of rudder pressure needed to keep aircraft climbing straight out....*

*—PNF reads checklist steps aloud while you listen to confirm he is making correct choices as checklist offers different procedures based on indications....*

*—Pitch?–adjust....*

*—Airspeed?—adjust....*

*—Heading?....*

*—Time to level off at the single engine level off height and order PNF to raise the flaps to minimize drag all the while keeping the plane level, on heading and accelerating....*
*—Pitch?....*
*—Heading?....*
*—Airspeed?....*
*—Once aircraft is cleaned-up (flaps up) continue climb to clearance altitude and begin maneuvering aircraft for landing....*
*—While flying, the PNF advises me of any visible anomalies and confirms steps in checklist with me. Checklist now completed. All fire indications out....*
*— Can we return to the airport we just departed? Is the runway long enough for a heavy single engine landing? Is the weather suitable for landing? Or must we plan to go somewhere else? We decide a return to departure airport is best course....*
*—ATC issues vectors (instructions to turn aircraft) for return approach*
*—Pilots prepare to brief return approach....*
*—Elapsed time from brake release on runway to this point? Approximately two minutes. Less than the time it takes most people to read it.*

All this information must be processed by the pilot flying the aircraft. Decisions must be made as to what happened? How can we fix it? If we can't fix it, what is our best course of action to get the aircraft safely back on the ground?—all the while flying the aircraft smoothly and deliberately. Even an experienced aviator flying an engine failed departure for the very first time in a new aircraft may be so busy that he barely hears his partner talking to him. This rapid onset of tasking is referred to by aviation instructors as "task overload" or "task saturation." Task overload is another reason another experienced aviator in the cockpit is worth his weight in gold when things get busy. After completion of training, these events become fairly routine.

During initial training and recurrent training, pilots experience a gamut of emergencies in the simulator. Captains are required to participate in a four-hour simulator training session every eighteen months as well as undergo a simulator check-ride during the same eighteen-month period.

In April, I climb into the "box" for a four-hour check ride and in October I do a training ride in the simulator covering the same areas as the check ride. In addition, I get a line check once a year, during which a company designated Check Airman observes me flying an actual flight with passengers. Furthermore, I am subject to FAA examiners hopping on my aircraft without notice, to evaluate my performance. With a $10,000 fine for any infraction and months off or even permanent license revocation as the result of any major violation of Federal Air Regulations (FARs), I am motivated to do the job right. In addition, I am required to get two flight physicals every year. All this is to ensure that the 50,000 people that I fly almost a quarter of a million miles each year, will get to their destinations safe and sound. I wish my family doctor was monitored as well as I am in his professional duties.

Increased training for pilots as well as detailed lessons that have been learned from previous accidents have further increased the margins of safety in aviation. Thirty years ago fatal accidents on commercial airliners occurred once in every 140 million miles flown. Today the figure is 1.4 billion miles flown per fatal accident—a ten-fold improvement in safety.

## Coffee or Orange Juice?

Flight Attendants have a credibility problem. Many passengers, and unfortunately some pilots, forget the Flight Attendants are actually part of the crew. Some passengers think the Flight Attendant's sole purpose is to hand out drinks and lift passengers' bags into the overhead bin. Some passengers never realize that Flight Attendants are actually highly trained professionals whose first and foremost job is making sure passengers get through their flight safely.

In a real emergency, Flight Attendants are the instruments the Captain will use to inform, instruct, and if necessary, evacuate you from the airplane. In the event the pilots become incapacitated after landing, the Flight Attendants are trained to direct you out of the aircraft. They train for emergencies and use mock-ups of real cabins and safety equipment annually. Their experience, judgment, and training will guide you out of danger should an emergency situation arise. Their commands during an emergency will literally lead you to safety. Handing out drinks is only a small part of their job.

Aside from the "brace" for impact commands and evacuation drills they practice, cabin crews are charged with a whole list of common sense rules developed by the FAA and airlines to help maximize the probability you get to your destination safely. Often these rules are handed out during boarding with little time to explain the "whys" behind the rules. Understandably, the passenger feels like a school kid being admonished by an overbearing teacher. However, when you think about the process, if Flight Attendants had to explain every rule imposed on every passenger, it would take hours to board the plane. To examine each would require a book in itself. (In Chapter 7, we'll look at the "whys" behind some of these rules.)

# Calling Mr. Fixit!

The pilots, crews, and the flying public would be grounded in short order without the talented people in aircraft maintenance. Aircraft are tremendously complex machines, usually pressing the state of the art of aviation technology, and they require knowledgeable technicians to keep them in the air.

Helicopters, for example, are comprised of thousands of individual parts, many of which are on a flight time or calendar life span. After so many hours, or so many months, the part has to be inspected and or replaced. The joke is, you can buy a 20-year-old helicopter and in reality, only the seats and fuselage are twenty years old. Everything else has been replaced. The same is true for many parts on a jetliner.

Jetliners are made for reliability and safety, and are inspected at very frequent intervals. The aircraft logbook is the official record of inspections and any maintenance that might be done on the aircraft. Even if nothing malfunctions, the log must be inspected once every seven days to make sure the paperwork reflecting any work or inspections done to the aircraft is accurate. Only then is the Airworthiness Release signed off by the mechanic. Without this preliminary paper review, the plane is grounded.

Every day several "walk around" visual inspections are done by the pilots who fly the aircraft. They check for wear on the tires, fluid leaks, and fluid levels for various systems on the jet, and overall condition outside the plane. The pilots look for possible damage to the outside of the aircraft from birds or vehicles that may have come into contact with the plane on the ground or inflight. These inspections can occur several times a day as different crews take their turn at the helm. Every seven days maintenance personnel do a similar inspection. Furthermore, the ground operations personnel (fuelers, baggage handlers, tug drivers, etc.) are always vigilant as the aircraft is parked at the gate and sing out if they see anything out of the ordinary. These workers see planes day in and day out. Something out of the ordinary stands out and they will notify the crew if anything is unusual.

Once inside the cockpit, pilots do a thorough cockpit pre-flight inspection, exercising various aircraft systems. Every eight months the control systems, hydraulic systems, and emergency equipment within the cockpit and cabin are inspected and tested by maintenance personnel. Once every 12 to 17 months, mechanics open up all panels on the aircraft and pore over all structure, plumbing and wiring with a fine-toothed comb. They look for cracks, leaks, and corrosion or wear not readily visible with the naked eye or any other signs of a potential problem. Finally, every three to five years, each airplane is completely disassembled, inspected and put back together. Anything and everything that can be unbolted from the plane is removed and all portions of the airframe are inspected in minute detail. I've been on a plane during this check and the process is not pretty. The interior is unrecognizable as that of an aircraft. During this major inspection, any cracks that are discovered are repaired and all systems are returned to like-new status, or entirely replaced, as necessary.

"Cracks are repaired, you say?" That's right. Cracks are a normal part of the life of an airplane. The aluminum skin of the plane comes under various flight and pressurization stresses and these factors can produce cracks in the skin. Using special equipment, the maintenance technicians can identify minute fractures that would be invisible to the naked eye before they pose a problem. Areas where cracks form are layered with a new overlay of aluminum skin to take the flight stresses and eliminate any further cracks. That's the good thing about a plane with a long history of service like the Boeing 737. We know from experience exactly where cracks will form in a new plane just off the assembly line, and we know about when in the life of the aircraft they will begin to appear. Maintenance crews watch these areas for the first sign of any problems.

High engine reliability has become commonplace now through new manufacturing techniques and materials. Engines are now run on the wing almost to failure, and the engine manufacturers and maintenance crews predict this failure with great precision. "Nearly to failure? How can they do that safely?"

Every day the engine flies, a log is taken of various engine parameters and kept on file in a computer. Should any parameter start to change, the computer signals a potential problem for maintenance to examine. Periodically, a flexible viewing scope called a borescope is inserted into the inner parts of the engine, through special removable panels designed just for this intimate inspection. A suspect engine might be borescoped weekly or even daily to check a potential problem. In addition, oil samples can be taken and analyzed. Any failure of a bearing or internal part will show traces of the metal that the part is made from, in the engine oil, well before the part fails. With this kind of monitoring, engines no longer need to be removed at some arbitrary time limit. As long as they are monitored and remain within very tight limits, the engine remains in service. Some engines of the same model have operated two to three times as long as others that have been removed due to some indicated problem. Because of great strides in monitoring technology, engine reliability has never been better, and that greatly improves safety.

We have covered how the crews prepare for the inevitable malfunction as well as how maintenance works hard to catch little problems before they get to be big ones. Inevitably though, incidents of malfunction occur in flight.

The next chapter deals with what effect those malfunctions really have on planes and on you, the passenger. We will also examine the mindset of the pilot. If you cringe at the thought of being helplessly "out of control" strapped as a passenger, you should be comforted to know what is going through the head of the two or three people up front, who literally are in control of you, your family, and friends as you fly.

If you really want to know, and you should, turn the page and read about "When Things Go Wrong."

*Gusty winds buffeted a commuter plane during a landing, giving the passengers a scare. Much to everyone's relief, they touched down safely and taxied to their parking spot where ramp agents were anxiously waiting. Unfortunately, in their haste, the ramp agents neglected to lock the mobile stairway firmly in place. It was an octogenarian who got off the plane first. Walking cane in hand, he stepped on the stairway. Almost simultaneously, the wind gusted to gale force, propelling the man and stairs across the ramp towards the terminal. We watched helplessly as they sailed over the concrete and crashed into a chain-link fence— whereupon the elderly gentleman stepped off unscathed, tipped his hat to the bystanders and said, "Best damn service I've ever had!"*

# Six:

# When Things Go Wrong

**Remember** the old T.V. show "Voyage to the Bottom of the Sea"? Whenever there was a major problem, the submarine would rock back and forth. Actually, the actors ran from wall to wall as the camera tilted back and forth. Hollywood knows how to show *ACTION*!

Take just about any movie with an airliner in it, and if something goes wrong, "BANG! Oh my God we are in a dive and the plane is going faster and faster STRAIGHT DOWN!" Well, you know the rest. You have seen the story a zillion times.

Thank goodness the obligatory screaming dives, giant dinosaurs, and real-live cartoon people all reside in the minds of the Hollywood professionals who think these things up. Otherwise, movies would get pretty boring. On any flight with me though, keep that kind of excitement limited to the inflight movie or a good book. Looking out the window is plenty of excitement for me. Seeing the Grand Canyon at sunrise, or Niagara Falls by moonlight, now that's pretty neat. Flying is still magic to me, and I still get a charge out of looking at the scenery going by. You should too.

PSSTTT. SECRET INFO HERE! Window seats are THE seats to have. Aisles are great if you fly frequently and have seen the country, or need access to the restroom, but I prefer a window. People with window seats are always relaxed, because they are informed. They know when the plane is about to take-off or land. They know why the airplane is rumbling, because they can see the spoilers up in flight. They also know something about the weather outside. If you don't like flying, trust me; get a window seat and make yourself look out the window for five minutes. Chances are, your nose will hurt by the end of the flight from pressing against the window. I have spent many flights seated next to anxious flyers and getting them to look out the window calms them down nearly every time.

When I am the Captain in command, I want my passengers to know they can participate in the flight to any extent they wish, be it by looking out the window, or enjoying the inflight entertainment, food, their choice: Whatever makes them comfortable. Or, if a person prefers, he or she can wake up from a nap as we touch down. The choice is solely theirs. Relaxed travel is the name of the game. I want the passenger to rest assured that he or she need not worry until I come on the P.A. and say "Folks, it's *time* to start worrying."

Some thoughtless pilots want to keep the passengers as minimally informed as possible. I feel a large part of my job as pilot involves keeping the passengers informed regarding pertinent aspects of our flight such as routing, weather, and arrival time. In the event of weather, I tell them exactly what we are up against and how we plan to deal with the situation. I would rather inform the most attuned of them, rather than treat them all like sixth graders. Those interested, and with questions or concerns, will pay attention and genuinely appreciate timely information. Those with no interest probably never listen to announcements anyway. I get more thanks than complaints with this approach.

I really am saddened when I open the newspaper up to some headline about a jetliner that blew a tire on landing or had some similarly mundane type of a malfunction, and during a non-emergency evacuation, somebody got hurt. With most emergencies, your biggest risk of danger is by going down the emergency slide. I am very serious about that. I am also concerned that in some minor malfunction, like a blown tire or similar problem, people really think their lives are on the line. Remember: The pilots up front are concerned about their own well being too. If they tell you not to worry, it is a good sign they feel they have the tools and experience to deal with the matter at hand. Take their suggestion and try to relax.

## Trust Your Pilot—An example of how an "Emergency" should work—

A Captain friend of mine took off one morning on a short flight from Las Vegas to Burbank. As they prepared to land in Burbank, upon lowering the landing gear, indications were that the left main gear had not extended correctly. A small part had failed inside the landing gear, jamming a tire against the lower portion of the fuselage during gear extension. This had never happened before in the 30 plus year history of the plane in over 90 million gear retractions—a highly unusual incident. Because the flight was near it's destination, in good weather, but with little extra fuel, it meant the crew had only a short time in which to decide how to resolve the problem. The Captain told the passengers about the situation, and kept them up-to-date as they tried different attempts to remedy the problem. Finally, after coordinating by radio with the airline maintenance technicians, the airline training center folks, airline management and Boeing, it was time to go ahead and land on the right main wheel and the nose tire. The left engine would serve as the left main landing gear. No big deal, Boeing designed the engine pylon to support the weight of the plane in just such an occurrence. After landing, inspection determined that the gear would not have come down by itself no matter what the crew had done.

The Captain informed the passengers of his decision, and most of them took it fine. Some however, after years of Hollywood and media conditioning, literally thought they were about to die. One strong young man seated by an emergency exit window, was asked by the Flight Attendants, as required by FAA regulation, if he was ready to respond to commands to open the hatch if necessary upon landing. He said, "No. I don't think I can." He was reseated away from the exit, and a strong, but much smaller young lady volunteered to take his place at the exit. The plane landed, and except for sparks made by the grinding engine pod, the landing was absolutely normal. Well, almost.

The passengers performed just as they were instructed. Once the plane ground to a halt, they let out with a cheer. They were told to remain seated until the crash response folks looked the plane over, to confirm no evidence of fire. After a "thumbs-up" from the head of the crash team, the pilots determined that, due to the unusual attitude of the plane sitting on its left engine, an air stair (portable steps) wheeled up to the plane might not work. Due to the lack of landing gear on the left side, the rear of the plane was much lower than usual. Instead, the Captain ordered a calm, relaxed evacuation out the back of the plane.

The Flight Attendants deployed an escape slide on the lower left rear side and began calmly helping people out of the plane. Halfway through the evacuation, as the remaining people were mostly toward the rear of the aircraft, the plane started to settle on the tail. (Voyage to the Bottom of the Runway!) The passengers stayed calm and did exactly what the crew told them to do, and everyone evacuated in good shape.

After exiting the back door, the passengers were bussed in small groups to the terminal. Upon arrival there, the Captain gathered the passengers and thanked them for being so calm and doing exactly what they were told. The passengers were nervous, but they performed exactly as instructed. Unfortunately, some of the folks thought the situation was far worse than the reality. Passenger safety is always foremost in the minds of the crew.

Don't think I am saying the pilots and crew weren't nervous too. They were doing something they had trained for, but had never actually seen for real. For sure, there was a small margin for error in this situation, but the crew was highly experienced, and their training had been superb. They applied good common sense with good advice, and the result was virtually no damage to the plane, or injury to the passengers.

Later, after the passengers were taken care of, the plane was jacked up on the runway, the landing gear lowered and, upon inspection, only the thrust reverser mounted on the back of the engine was damaged (read: ground to hamburger). The engine, which had been shutdown as a precaution just prior to landing, was in perfect order. After a precautionary engine change and a swap of the left main landing gear, the plane was back in service two days later.

## Pilots Are People Too!

Just remember, pilots are the first people on the scene of an airplane accident. I have had many, obviously nervous, people tell me as they walked down the jetway, "Make sure we get there safe and sound." Or another one is, "Are you gonna fly safe today?" I answered one person's question by saying, "Gosh darn, I was gonna fly really crazy, but now I guess I have to be really safe." I suppose that was not the most professional answer, but after my reply sunk in, the young woman clearly wished she had never spoken such a ludicrous line. I reassured her anyway. Hey, I'm on this plane too! I've got a wife and a daughter at home waiting for me. Do you think I came to work just to risk my life for you? No way! I want to get you to your destination safe and happy, and then get back home to my family.

Since I began flying many years ago, I have avoided any act, which might be considered even remotely reckless. I take the charge of my crew and passengers very seriously. I have over 16,000 hours of flying time without bending one piece of metal. I am proud of that record, and I want it to continue. I represent just a mid-level experience pilot too. There are pilots out there with upwards of 30,000 to 40,000 hours of flying experience, and there's a reason they have lasted so long.

There is an old saying in aviation: "There are 'Old Pilots' and there are 'Bold Pilots'. But, there are no 'Old Bold' pilots." Put another way: He who scares and runs away, lives to fly another day. As I said in a previous chapter, the ability to make good decisions and plan ahead is the foundation of a good aviator.

Shortly after I graduated from flight school in the Air Force, I was visited by a former student friend en route to his fighter assignment in Korea. I was flying T-43s (the military version of the Boeing 737) at the time, and he wanted to see my plane. Sitting in the cockpit, Harry asked me, "Wow, don't you think about all those folks in the back while you are flying?" I told Harry, "I figure if I make it okay, they'll make it okay." That's the motto I have lived by for over twenty years.

Remember, your pilots are very experienced and very cautious. They don't *want* to do anything stupid.

Now, I'm not going to shred my credibility by saying that pilots in the past have not done stupid things. Some have, over the history of aviation, and that's why we have better rules now for how we go about our business. Certainly our training has improved as well. We have used previous accidents as lessons in an attempt to preclude these same errors from creeping in and affecting safety. Will it ever be 100% safe? Someday, perhaps.

As long as humans are at the controls, you will occasionally have mistakes, but humans operating the aircraft sure beat the alternative. Believe me, you don't want a machine flying you. You want a pilot in the loop, involved with the task at hand. When the machine goes goofy, you want the pilot to be able to punch off the computer and take over. Anyone who has any computer experience can certainly understand this logic. That's why Boeing, and most other manufacturers allow the pilot to take command over the computers.

There was a rumor out many years back that the Japanese had perfected a system whereby a jet could taxi itself along taxiways to and from the runway without the aid of the pilot. The aircraft were reportedly equipped with sensors to follow wires buried in the taxiways and runways of some Japanese airports. Discussing this new angle on aviation technology over lunch with fellow coworkers, I pushed this technology one logical step further. Some jets, once programmed by the pilots, can fly themselves from take-off to touchdown without the pilot touching the controls. If this new technology allowed the planes to find their way to and from the runway, technologically speaking, the pilot position could be reduced to one individual in the cockpit, solely as a system monitor acting, only if a problem arose. Upon hearing this news, my fellow pilots and I pondered this scenario, and then after a minute of thoughtful cogitation, laughed out loud at the absurdity of the thought. The only thing scarier than a machine doing all the flying, is a pilot taking over with limited proficiency after not having touched the controls in eons. Now *that's* a *scary* thought.

# Dealing With Emergencies—What's a Good Malfunction?

To just put out a list of "These are OK problems, these are not as good and for these, break out the worry beads…" wouldn't make much sense. Incidents are always situationally dependent. Finding a flat tire on your car in your garage is a problem, but much less so than having the tire blow out at high speed, in heavy traffic, in driving rain. An extreme example, but you get the idea.

System failures on a jetliner are rare, but as you already know, most systems are backed up by secondary (and often tertiary) layers of systems designed to operate with little impact on the control and operation of the aircraft. Certain problems may require cutting the flight short of the destination, and based on experience and intervening variables, the Captain will make the most conservative decision possible to get you, and the crew, safely back on the ground.

Some malfunctions, a pressurization problem for example, might mean continuing the flight, but in a modified way. After a pressurization system malfunction, you may be able to descend to a lower altitude and continue if you have enough fuel left. No big deal. The problem is, planes burn more fuel at lower altitudes, and an unplanned drop to a lower altitude on a longer flight might mean that you have to make a gas stop short of your destination. An example of a modified, but totally safe flight continued to completion despite a malfunction. While we are talking about pressurization problems, I mentioned earlier that I had experienced one as a passenger.

## Pressurization Problems

The safety briefings required by the FAA and given by Flight Attendants mentions the masks falling from the overhead bin above.

I have been through a decompression event and they are nothing to be worried about.

I was en route to Korea on a C-5 transport while in the Air Force, to see my wife who was also a service member and stationed in Korea. The C-5 is a HUGE cargo plane, and the passenger section is on the upper deck near the tail. We were cruising along after lunch and I started to notice my ears popping. I also noticed the large pressurization equalization doors in the back wall of the cabin starting to swing out, signaling that the air was leaking out of the plane in a hurry. At my feet were some twenty bags of potato chips in a box left over from lunch. As I looked at the bags they started to pop, from the over-pressure within. Actually they popped from the under-pressure from outside! After reading Chapter 9, "Aerospace Physiology," you will know as much about pressurization as I do. About that time I was hit on the head by the familiar yellow "margarine cup" of the passenger oxygen system. I put the odd looking, ill fitting, flimsy plastic cup over my big nose and laughed. "Now this is a hoot, how am I supposed to breath out of this thing?" I was spoiled by fancy pilot breathing gear we have in the cockpit.

As I had practiced many times myself, the pilots throttled the engines to idle, and the plane began a quick descent to a lower altitude. The hurry is in order to get down to an altitude where oxygen isn't necessary before the emergency passenger oxygen systems run out. This rush to descend also minimizes the passenger's exposure to an under-pressurized environment. The passenger oxygen system needs only to provide oxygen for about 10 minutes, which is plenty enough time to descend to where oxygen is no longer needed. My depressurization experience was all calm and relaxed. And no, my little green oxygen bag never did inflate, just as the Flight Attendants mention in their pre-take-off briefing. This depressurization incident was really no big deal. That is, until we landed and I found out it would be two days before they fixed the plane: Only then could I could get to Korea to finally see my wife who I hadn't seen in four months.

## Engine Problems

In a previous chapter we discussed in detail what happens when an engine fails. Once the plane gets away from the ground you are nearly out of the woods. If the weather is clear enough for the pilots to make a visual approach back to the airport, you are in sterling shape. If you happen to be in weather and an instrument approach is necessary, this will mean flying a bit longer. Rest assured, in the simulator, we always have terrible weather when we have an engine problem. We have practiced this maneuver many times, flying our way back to the airport solely on instruments and seeing the runway only seconds before we land.

If you are up at cruise and an engine goes to sleep, the pilots have tons of time to try a restart, or plan on nearby airfields to divert into. Remember, the plane is designed to lift off the runway, fully loaded and climb away safely from the ground with one engine inoperative. Even at a moderate altitude an engine failure is much less critical of an event than the name implies. The airplane goes downhill with virtually no thrust from the engines during routine descents. And, the aircraft is quite capable of going around should the landing need to be aborted for some reason. I have had four separate engine failures in all my years of flying, and all were on departure or at the top of climb. The return was totally uneventful. Remember, the plane is designed to be flown with less than the full complement of engines running. That is one reason the aircraft manufacturers install more than one motor on airliners.

An engine fire is more problematic. As I mentioned earlier, fire *inside* the engine is a good thing, but when outside for more than a second, becomes a major concern. Every engine on a jet transport has a fire extinguisher bottle designed to extinguish fires should one erupt. Even the Auxiliary Power Unit (APU). These bottles of fire suppressant are very effective in shutting off oxygen to the fire and extinguishing the flames. The switch that arms these bottles also shuts off fuel, hydraulic, pneumatic, oil, and electrical connections isolating the motor and removing any extended source of fuel for combustion. If for some unfathomable reason the fire is still burning, the engine pylon itself may melt off, allowing the burning engine to fall free of the aircraft. Safety is one of the prime reasons engines are installed away from the fuselage or wing on pylons. Isolating the motor away from the aircraft not only helps during a fire but reduces noise and vibration as well. Once the engine is shutdown by the crew, there are no sources of fuel to burn, except for a couple of gallons of engine oil. I have never heard of a modern jet engine continuing to burn out of control. A very few specialized engine parts are made out of magnesium, a metal which will burn when heated to extreme temperatures. Occasionally, magnesium parts of the engine will burn brightly and eventually fall clear of the aircraft.

## Hydraulic or Electric Problems

I lump these two system malfunctions into the same topic because their effect is virtually identical. In both cases all important systems are "backed up" by secondary or tertiary level systems and the affect on aircraft performance or control is negligible. Lose a generator or a hydraulic system and after securing the wounded system, the pilots will most likely continue to the destination after a consideration of time remaining, weather considerations, and any other factors which might apply.

In the case of a total electrical failure, (a *very rare* occurrence) the aircraft is designed to operate on battery back up for a sufficient time to land at the nearest suitable airport. In the equally rare instance where total hydraulic failure occurs, most aircraft today are quite manageable solely by pilot muscle input to the flight control system. You may not experience the smoothest landing but you'll get down just fine. In the Air Force we used to practice "manual reversion," all-hydraulics-out, approaches to cloud layers in the practice areas. Flying the aircraft took a bit more muscle and finesse on the trim wheel but the task was quite manageable. Similar to a car that has experienced power steering failure, you are still operating the front wheel steering, only with your muscles instead of your fingertips.

## Take-off Aborts

In a previous chapter we covered weight concerns and how they impact our take-off preparation. In the event the pilot detects a problem and elects to discontinue the take-off, there must be enough room to stop. Simply put, an abort is termination of a take-off. Compared to what many experienced travelers have encountered, the braking mode during an abort is almost violent. Once the decision to abort is made it must be carried out without hesitation and with maximum effort. During these few seconds, the pilot's sole reason for existence is to stop the aircraft safely on the runway. To yield to comfort and brake gently only to find the runway end approaching rapidly is unacceptable.

The aircraft brakes and engines are used to stop the aircraft in the quickest possible manner. During this deceleration, the brakes mounted on the main wheels can absorb millions of foot-pounds of energy bringing the plane to a stop. This results in extreme heating of the brake assemblies. Occasionally, this heat buildup in the tire rim causes "fuse plugs," on the wheel rims, to melt. These plugs on the wheel rims let the air out of the tires, preventing the tires from popping due to heat buildup and the resulting overpressure inside the tire after the plane stops. In some extreme instances, the absorbed heat from braking will cause the brake assemblies to glow cherry red, and eventually the tires may ignite. Airliners are tested during certification to ensure they can come to a stop, and sit unaided by fire crews for fifteen minutes with their tires completely ablaze. The situation looks terrifying, but is just another aspect of the aircraft operation tested extensively during certification. If you are on a heavily loaded aircraft that aborts at high speed, you may see smoke coming from under the wings, even flames. Rest assured this is perfectly normal and expected. Fire crews are en route to your aircraft and will be dousing your wheels down should the need arise. They won't be flying you out on this aircraft until maintenance completely inspects the tires and brakes. This inspection is required before the next flight.

## Technical Stuff:

> *Another source of smoke is a new brake assembly. As we mentioned earlier, brakes on aircraft are similar to the brakes on cars except that they have many "rotors" versus the one rotor or "disc" in a car brake. Jetliner brakes wear out just like automobile brakes and are periodically replaced. When maintenance technicians assemble these, the brake components get contaminated by small amounts of oil or grease. As the brake heats under normal use, this small amount of oil and grease heats up as well. This, in combination with the new brake pad material, produces noticeable smoke during the first few flights while taxiing on the ground. Once the brake assembly gets heated and the foreign material burns off, the smoke eventually stops. You may see this smoke emanating from the wheels on your aircraft or another nearby.*

# Flight Controls

Flight control issues are one other area that might generate some concern on the part of the passenger (see Figures 23 and 24).

Landing with no flaps just means you land at a higher speed, which may require the pilots to choose another airport if your destination airport runway is too short to accommodate the higher landing speeds. If one of the flaps jams and makes the plane roll unexpectedly, the pilots have procedures to deal with this too; just leave the flaps where they are and land at the nearest suitable airport.

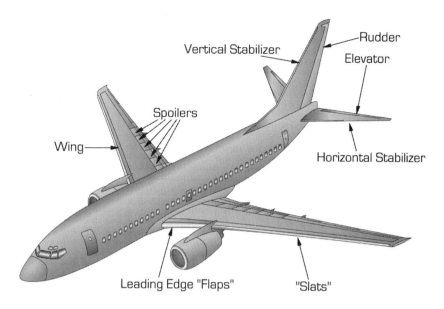

*Figure 23. Flight Control Surfaces*

# Boeing 737 Rudder Anomalies

In that I have spent so much time talking about the Boeing 737, you might be wondering about my feelings on the rudder issue. If you are not familiar with the details, let me explain.

The Boeing 737 has reportedly had a few instances that have been described as "spontaneous and uncommanded rudder input." What does that mean?

The rudder is what keeps the nose of the plane going straight and when an engine fails, this is the one control that makes flying the plane possible with a thrust imbalance. Without the rudder, in an engine failure situation, you are nearly helpless to stop the nose from yawing as the thrust of the operating engine pushes the nose toward the failed engine. The rudder is the movable rear part of the vertical stabilizer on the tail and is essentially like the rudder on a boat.

Two accidents years ago involving the Boeing 737 look suspiciously like they may be involved with this rudder phenomenon. One involved a United 737 on approach to Colorado Springs, and the

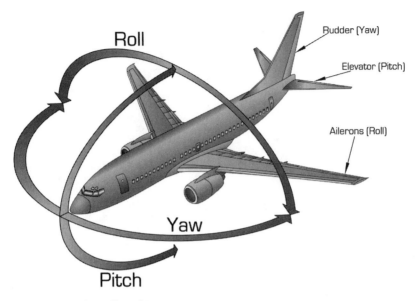

*Figure 24. Pitch, Roll and Yaw*

other involved a USAir 737 on approach to Pittsburgh. In both accidents the rudder actuator was examined very closely. In the USAir
case, under very peculiar situations, the actuator was found to act
abnormally. Investigators had to freeze the rudder actuator, and then
apply a torch to heat a portion of the device to cause the rudder actuator to malfunction. How this might happen in flight is unknown.
Boeing studied the problem intently, and decided to totally redesign
the rudder actuator to preclude any future possibility of abnormal
behavior. All 737 rudder actuators in use by airlines have been replaced
with new, redesigned units.

I have never encountered this problem in over 18 years of flying
the 737, and I feel confident that should this problem ever occur, I
could resolve the problem and land safely. I trust that plane with my
life and the lives of my family and friends. Remember, a 737 takes off
every six seconds. If this problem occurred frequently, we would see it
daily or weekly in the news media. Newer 737s, built since the
mid-1980s, have a hull loss record which is four times better than the
industry average. (A hull loss is an aircraft damaged beyond repair.)

Older model 737s, referred to as "Classic" models, equipped with the original rudder actuator design have safely transported nearly 6 billion passengers over thirty years—an amount equal to the entire world population. The Classic family of 737s has flown over 91 million hours—the equivalent of flying 24 hours a day, seven days a week, for about 10,390 years. This is clearly a safe and proven aircraft design.

# Aircraft Evacuation

Some situations may require the passengers to exit the aircraft immediately after stopping on the runway, either during take-off or during landing. Whether or not an evacuation is necessary will be a decision made by the flight crew and relayed to you immediately after landing. Remain seated and quiet until this information is passed on to you either by the pilots after they bring the aircraft to a stop or relayed through the Flight Attendants. You may be directed to remain seated until the fire team examines the aircraft and relays that information back to the pilots by radio. In a case where the pilots have become incapacitated, the Flight Attendants will make that decision alone. Except in a dire situation where fire or heavy smoke is present, DO NOT INITIATE AN EVACUATION WITHOUT DIRECTION FROM THE CREW.

Years back on a Boeing 727, an APU oil seal failed—this is a normal occurrence over time. As the APU shut down, the last bit of exhaust smoked quite a bit as the APU turbine wound down. The APU exhaust was located in the wing right next to passenger windows. Without any crew knowledge, a passenger decided the plane was on fire and initiated his own evacuation while the plane was taxiing out for take-off. Imagine the scene, an airliner taxiing along with several passengers out on the wing. Once the Captain was notified, those on the wing were lucky they didn't fall off as the plane came to a stop. Fortunately, no one was injured in this incident. There was absolutely no threat to the passengers inside the aircraft during this event.

Passengers must listen for emergency instructions from the crew and follow their direction promptly and exactly to avoid injury or unnecessary delay for passengers evacuating behind them. Often the safest place during an emergency is inside an aircraft, even in cases of fire. I recently watched a training video of an airliner with an engine fire. The plane landed uneventfully and was met by the fire response team immediately after coming to a stop on the runway. The crew ordered the passengers to remain seated while the fire team dealt with the fire. Magnesium parts burned brightly on the engine as the firefighters doused the engine with water. After a couple minutes, the fire team had the fire extinguished and the aircraft taxied to the gate. Had the passengers been evacuated, they would have faced confusion in the darkness; knee deep fire foam and water as well as fast moving emergency vehicles on the runway, not to mention injuries resulting from incorrect techniques while sliding down the emergency escape slides. Your crew will tell you what to do. Wait for their command.

In the event the crew directs you to evacuate, do so calmly and quickly. DO NOT DELAY TO COLLECT PERSONAL POSSESSIONS! LEAVE EVERYTHING YOU BROUGHT ABOARD! Proceed to the nearest exit, if possible. Some evacuations may be away from the hazard and the crew may direct you to only evacuate from the front, rear or only one side. In any case, if you are the first person to arrive at an exit, look outside for hazards (fire, dense smoke, or other hazards) before opening the exit. Once you determine the exit path is clear, open the exit.

**Doors:** Each doorway (the 737 has four, other planes may have six or more) has an emergency slide attached. By opening the door you automatically inflate the slide for that exit. Once the escape slide inflates in a few seconds, jump onto the slide being careful to clear the doorway threshold with your posterior. Jump down and out to clear the plane and land on the slide keeping your arms crossed over your chest to avoid getting burns on your hands should they get underneath your body or twist shoulders as you first impact the slide. Keep your shoes on (unless wearing spiked heels which may damage the slide), as you will need them on the ground. The first people out should help stabilize the bottom of the slide and help people clear away from the bottom landing area as quickly as possible. The other passengers should move upwind and away from the aircraft watching closely for responding emergency vehicles. I would hate to successfully escape a burning aircraft only to be run over by a fire truck or other rescue vehicle maneuvering into position in smoke or fog!

**Overwing Escape Hatches:** The older type hatches on the 737 and many other planes opened inward and disconnect from the aircraft. The passenger opening this type hatch should cock the hatch at a slight angle after opening and throw the hatch out on the wing before exiting. Do not bring it inside the aircraft as it may block passengers who need that exit. (Women, don't be alarmed. The hatches weigh only about 50 pounds and you will be plenty motivated should the need arise.)

Newer hatches open outward automatically assisted by springs when activated. Remember to open these exits palm up so as to prevent being snatched out of the plane as the exit opens. With your palm up, your arm will hinge at the wrist and elbow comfortably. The newer hatches are clearly marked with pictorial instructions, which clearly show them opening up and away. Crews refer to these as "DeLorean doors" in a reference to the gull-wing doors used on some sports cars. Someday, all escape hatches will be of this design.

Once outside the overwing hatch, your route of exit is off the rear edge of the wing, sliding down the flaps like a kid on a steep slide. Part of the pilot's emergency evacuation checklist is ensuring the flaps are fully extended for just this event. Exit arrows are painted on the wing of most jetliners pointing you in the right direction. Again, conditions permitting, it is helpful if a couple of people stand on the ground below the flap helping people land and directing them away from the plane.

Emergency ground evacuations and their associated risks are weighed heavily by aircrews during emergencies. They will use their experience and training to direct you depending on the circumstances. Obeying their commands will ensure the best chance of survival for everyone on board.

# Failures Outside Your Aircraft

As a new student pilot, my least favorite "emergency" was contemplating a communication radio failure in the aircraft I was flying. The textbook answer involved flying the flight plan route exactly as previously cleared. En route, we would broadcast a "radio out" code via transponder, that device which broadcasts information to ATC radarscopes. Instead of my "license plate" number, I'd dial in the "radio out" symbol. Then I'd land as usual looking for the "green light" shone from the control tower indicating I was cleared to land. Most airliners have two or more radios so being totally without some means of communication is a rare occurrence. But, should the need arise, we would use the same procedures.

Air Traffic Control occasionally loses a radio and as you would imagine, they have back-up radios in most locations. If needed, some sectors of ATC can temporarily handle the adjoining sectors traffic while radio problems get resolved. The newest of these radios was built when I was in college and while they are fairly reliable, radio failures are a fairly common occurrence and rarely result in a delay. However, ATC radar failures virtually guarantee extensive ground delays.

As we discussed earlier, radar is what ATC uses to keep updated on aircraft position and speed. This is the primary tool ATC uses to keep aircraft separated from one another while flying in "controlled" airspace. If your aircraft is airborne in a sector that loses radar, the pilots resort to the old fashioned method of position reporting to let the controllers know where their aircraft is. Pilots verbally inform the ATC controllers as they pass points along the airway they are flying on. That takes care of the planes in the air. Due to the need for more spacing resulting from the less than precise nature of verbal position reporting, all aircraft still on the ground with flight plans through that airspace will encounter *guaranteed* delays.

Having covered these situations, I cannot imagine any other single noteworthy item really posing a problem to the flight that you ought to worry about. Infrequently, totally off-the-wall things happen which sound disastrous at first look, but turn out fine in the end. Here is a funny case in point.

106

Jim is a good friend of mine who instructs pilots in annual Emergency Procedures Training. Jim isn't a pilot, but he knows the intricacies that pilots face in their day-to-day job, and he's the perfect guy to teach recurrent FAA mandated emergency training. The training is done at each of the company's crew bases and this requires Jim to fly nearly as much as the pilots do themselves. Oddly, Jim is not a real "relaxed" passenger. He swears that knowing all of us pilots has *nothing* to do with his anxiety.

One night while returning to Dallas, Jim was seated on the right side of the plane just behind the wing. Dallas was covered with an unusual series of very thin cloud layers. Unbeknownst to the pilots, several large flocks of geese were in holding patterns between layers of clouds. (I am not making this up folks.) Birds, aware of the dangers of losing control in clouds will opt to hold, even overnight if necessary, until a way can be found out of the weather. How birds navigate at night I can't imagine, except that they must use starlight or moonlight as an "up" reference. How they do this at night between cloud layers is unknown. Fortunately, this is a fairly rare occurrence.

About five minutes from touchdown, Jim's plane popped through a layer of clouds, and in the headlights all that the pilots could see was a huge line of geese they were about to hit. As both pilots instinctively *ducked* under the dash, about five good size geese impacted the plane at over 250 miles per hour.

One pierced the skin of the fuselage, and caromed around the lower electronic equipment bay where it hit an emergency gear lowering cable, lowering one main landing gear. Another impacted the left wing, very close to the left engine, damaging a significant portion of the leading edge of the wing. One poor bird went straight into the right engine that Jim happened to be staring at right at that moment.

SHABOOOMMMMHHHhhhhhhhhhhh.

Jim watched the right engine core disintegrate in a huge red fireball illuminating the right side of the heads of those seated for several rows in front of him. As he stared at diminishing red flames coming out of the five million dollar motor, now reduced to that of a giant sparkler, his first thought was "There goes my profit-sharing for the year." The engine casing had performed perfectly, containing the rotating parts as they came loose, and directing them out the rear of the engine.

In the cockpit, the Captain and his First Officer were faced with their own red glow, that of nearly every red light in the cockpit (Green Light—Good; Red Light—Bad) With the runway in sight they opted to quickly take care of the engine fire, and then land the plane in the quickest manner possible. By the time they landed, many passengers were still unaware of the magnitude of what had happened.

The point of this story is simply to illustrate that despite how we train for malfunctions and system failures, at times incidents happen we could never have planned for. Faced with several serious malfunctions simultaneously, the Captain and his First Officer in this example used good airmanship, common sense, and a focus on the important task at hand—continuing to FLY THE AIRPLANE all the way to the ground, to safely extricate their passengers and crew from possible peril. Rather than waste valuable time running extensive checklists, the pilots in this example took care of items they had seen in training from memory and left the rest for the maintenance folks on the ground. This is another essence of a good pilot, knowing which problems are important and which are mere distractions. Experience is what allows a pilot to prioritize when things get busy. Furthermore, this example shows that even when faced with multiple emergencies, as long as the plane is still flying, you are in darned good shape.

## Bird Strikes

After the preceding story, you probably have a new worry about suicidal killer birds looking to take out your jet engines. I must point out that the episode I described was very unusual. Aircraft are designed to take bird strikes. The cockpit windows are about an inch thick and made of very strong plastic, sandwiched between layers of glass. They are electrically heated to give them more flexibility, and are designed to withstand the impact of a bird traveling at 400 miles per hour. ("But Captain Ray, how many birds can fly 400 mph?" *Think about it!*) The engines are especially engineered to deal with the inevitable bird ingestion. The fan blades, the large ones visible on the front of most jet engines, are made of a phenomenal metal that bends like soft plastic on impact, and then reverts to its original shape. The internal compressor blades are extra tough and protected by the spinner on the front of the engine which is shaped to deflect water or other material past the turbine inlet without ingesting material into the motor. Frozen birds and all manner of materials are blasted by cannon into engines during testing to ensure the motors will continue to operate. Films of this testing are truly *amazing* to watch and really build confidence in the integrity and reliability of the engines—and their ability to gobble up errant things and keep running.

In the very rare occurrence when a small bird penetrates the core of the motors turbine section, the bird is instantly incinerated in the tremendous heat and pressure inside the engine. The bird remains usually passes through the engine with little noticeable effect, except the disgusting smell inside the aircraft of burning oily feathers. Remember, compressed air is bled off the engine core (just prior to adding fuel and a spark), and this compressed air powers the air conditioning system. Any oily residue from a bird ingestion will show up as a "fishy" smell inside the aircraft within seconds of the event.

In those ultra-rare instances when a motor is smacked head-on in the turbine section by a large bird, the engine may continue to run at a reduced thrust setting. Should it eventually disintegrate, as in previous example with Jim watching, the engine case is designed to contain the disintegration and the hot pieces of metal will simply blow out the back of the motor. The pilots will isolate the fuel, hydraulics, and other systems going to the engine, and then discharge an engine fire extinguisher bottle to squelch any residual fire. The plane simply continues flying on the remaining engine(s). Remember, planes are equipped with *extra* motors. The loss of one is not a fatal event.

Don't misread my light tone regarding the discussion of birdstrikes as something I take lightly. I am in total awe of my feathered friends in the air and I will take great steps to avoid hitting them if time and space permit. I consider myself an aviator but nowhere near the aviator that is the smallest sparrow. Airports are often great hunting or nesting grounds for fowl. Many times they appear out of nowhere leaving no chance for me to avoid them. I trespass into their realm and on the rare occurrence when our paths meet, it leaves me with sorrow knowing another of nature's creatures is gone. As a pilot, what I do only approximates what they are born to do.

The point of this rambling discussion was not to bore you with facts or scare you with "war" stories. Hopefully you now understand some of the planning, training and design features that go into making commercial aviation the safest form of transportation in the world. In addition, I hope you come away with the understanding that the pilots and crews of the planes you fly on are also human.

We repeatedly do an unbelievably complex and demanding job in a very professional manner. Most of us try to have a good sense of humor while doing our jobs. Our whole reason for existence is to get you safely from Point A to Point B. Without you, the customers, we pilots would be driving bulldozers or selling real estate. Ours is truly a partnership.

As a pilot I want you to feel confident in knowing that my brothers and sisters in this profession are highly experienced, and highly trained for the tasks we perform. We learn from other's experiences as well as our own so that we may do our jobs better.

In that we take our jobs very seriously, (though we take ourselves much less seriously at times), rest assured we work very hard to provide you with a safe and comfortable means of transportation. The fact that you bought this book, and are interested in what goes on within the air transport system, means you can intelligently converse with an employee and ask questions about things that concern you. If that person can't answer your question, they should direct you to someone who can.

I congratulate you on taking the initiative to learn about this business. There is nothing sadder than fear in isolation, fostered by ignorance. The term "ignorant" has taken on such a negative connotation, but the word "ignorance" merely means "without knowledge." In something so complex as the system I have tried to describe, the lack of knowledge is clearly understandable on your part. I'd be ignorant about your job in computers, farming, particle physics, advanced mathematics, the law, real estate, or whatever you do. Nowadays with the increasing complexity of things, we are all going to have to admit that in some areas we are truly "without knowledge." At least on this topic you have taken the time to learn and for that you deserve praise.

Now, assuming nothing blows up, burns off, or quits on your plane, let me give you some tips on how to deal with the really scary part of this business: The passenger sitting *next* to you.

*A peppery woman at the airline ticket counter was complaining about the delay in the departure of her flight. "Young man," she snapped at the reservations clerk, "the way you people run this airline, a witch on a janitor's broom could get there faster."*

*"Madam," the clerk said, with just a hint of a smile, "the runways are clear."*

# Seven:

# Keeping Your Sanity

**At** first thought, you might think that if God had meant for us to travel very far, he would have put wheels on our feet, and made the earth smooth and flat for those wheels to roll on. Or maybe he would have given us wings to fly on, so we could skip the whole skating thing. In reality, we have the best of all possible options. Our planet is shielded in an atmosphere that is light enough to breathe, yet is strong enough to hold up a jet full of passengers. Armed with intelligence and the ever versatile opposable thumb, we have fashioned vehicles that let us leave the earth for a time and travel very long distances, very, very quickly. It is a truly eloquent solution.

However we do it, traveling is often a traumatic experience, and I should know; I spend two or three nights a week in motels around the country. In the past 15 years at my airline, I have spent almost 1,700 nights away from home. You might think that by now I would be used to traveling but I have learned that you never really *ever* do. Dorothy was right: There's no place like home.

Since this book deals with traveling by air, I thought I'd offer a few tips to help make your trip more enjoyable. First and foremost: Some people make their own troubles—avoid this.

I mentioned in the last chapter that the guy seated next to you was the scariest part of this business. Let me clarify that statement.

In my experience, 95 percent of the people traveling on airlines are just super. They rarely complain, even when faced with delays or disruptions and once the facts are explained they usually soldier on admirably in the face of adversity. Many of these folks are experienced travelers who have seen it all. After all, does getting angry at the weather make any sense?

About four percent of travelers are upset for some reason. Their ticketing has been goofed up. Their luggage was checked to Timbuktu. They missed their connecting flight. Whatever the reason, the system has failed them, and they are understandably peeved and want to bring this problem to someone's attention. I like people like this because they mostly want to see someone empathize with their predicament. Perhaps I cannot solve their problem, but I might be able to somehow make it better. That's where customer service comes into play. Making excuses does not do a thing towards resolving their problem. In many cases, the damage is done; a helping hand is what they need. My job is to try and minimize further damage, and let the passenger know we are truly sorry things happened this way. My usual question is, "How can I make things better?" This usually relaxes the passenger, and we often part with smiles.

That leaves the final one percent of people. These are people your mother never told you about.

These folks create raucous confrontations with Flight Attendants for whatever reason, usually as a distraction from the fact that they are flying in a plane—something many of them are deathly afraid of doing. Or, they think by creating some big bogus brouhaha, they mistakenly think they can get some compensation from the airline, like free tickets.

Others in this group are just plain rude. They change their infant's diapers in mid-cabin for all to experience, and then leave the diaper under the seat. They let their kids totally trash the area they are seated in, including grinding cookies or crackers into the floor. They must think we tip the plane on its tail and hose it out between flights. I bet they'd be upset if I came over to their place and wasted *their* living room. Others open overhead bins and, as they rummage about, carelessly drop heavy objects on passengers seated below. These people simply do not care about their fellow traveler. They demand the rights that apply to them, but ignore the fact they impinge on the same rights held by their fellow travelers.

A few people are extremely loud and obnoxious, often manhandling female Flight Attendants by pinching them or pulling their uniforms to get their attention. Once in awhile, we encounter fellow travelers with severe hygiene dysfunction syndrome. The term "soap" is not in their vocabulary. Many are oblivious to anything not immediately before them, like the back of the backpack slung over their shoulder which, nearly decapitates each aisle seated passenger as it bumps down seatbacks while they mindlessly look for a seat. Many are simply not "aware" of what is going on around them.

These are but mild cases of "the unwashed one percent." Public decency laws and good taste prohibits me from detailing the really gross behavior. You wouldn't believe what occasionally happens in flight, but rest assured, there is a whole "*nuther*" world out there that our moms never told us about. Armed with this cruel immutable fact of nature, let us see how we can get the most out of our travel experience, even if we run into one or more of these people. Also, some tips on how not to run the risk of being confused as a "one percenter."

# The Golden Rule

The first and foremost rule most people try to operate under is: Treat others as you'd like to be treated. This doesn't mean you can't be upset if some travel employee has dropped the ball and goofed up your travel plans. Just remember: Be dignified. Get to the point without yelling and if you are getting nowhere with this person, simply ask to see a supervisor or some other person before you reach critical mass and your head explodes. Most travel service employees aren't on a mission to make your trip miserable. Stuff happens and as my Operations Agent friend Frank say's "Okay folks—this is life. Let's just deal with it and get on with things." Life's too short to get bent at every little "booger" on the windshield. Save up for the big ones.

And, when approached by employees honestly trying to do their job with at least a shred of compassion, try to comply as best you can with their demands and remember: They are people too. This may be

This is Your Captain Speaking

their sixth flight of the day or their tenth hour of work. A long hard day at work is no excuse to be surly but put yourself in their shoes. If you think they might be able to help you even though you are mad-as-hell-and-not-gonna-take-it-anymore, drop your anger and frustration for a minute. Just act human, describe your predicament, and the person with the power to solve your dilemma will probably empathize with you and bend over backwards. You always catch more flies with honey than vinegar. Remember, regardless of what the youths of today are trying to tell us, respect is earned. There are no shortcuts to respect. Imagine what a nicer place the world would be if more people dropped their attitudes and simply empathized with one another, now and then.

Now, for those airline employees who are way over the line, rude, or just plain socially reprehensible pigs, get their name if possible, and simply write the airline. Letters to my company *have* an impact and even if the employee explains his or her way out of termination or time off, the letter will go in their file. Should this happen again, a record of incidents indicates a trend and they'll get hammered should this behavior continue. If their poor display of personal interaction skills was indeed a lapse of judgment, they will work extra hard in the future knowing that letter is in their file and they'll straighten up. If they don't care, the letter you write may save the company—and the next passenger, the pain of a rude employee. Just remember most airlines want the employee's side of the story as well. Armed with facts and honest emotion, you'll at least convey your concerns, and hopefully spare someone else from re-experiencing the same incident.

Now, put the shoe on the other foot. Say you are boarding a plane, which is late, and you want a magazine from the overhead bin at the front of the plane. The Flight Attendant points out the obvious fact that boarding has ground to a halt while you try to decide whether to read *Rolling Stone* or *Reader's Digest*. Don't wail back at her. If looks could kill, those trying to get to their seat behind you would have instantly vaporized you for blocking their way. Maybe getting a magazine at a newsstand before boarding would be a better idea. Or, perhaps getting up once the plane is at cruise and the seatbelt sign is switched off. Just think ahead. Be aware of yourself and those around you. Use common sense, but remember: The customer is not always right. If you don't believe me just ask another customer.

I try to lead my life like I drive my car. If I can drive without having to cause any other drivers to alter their speed or direction, then I have operated my car successfully. Life doesn't always work that way, but at least I try. If more people took this approach to life, think how much nicer the world would be. Courtesy is a lost art in this day and age. Be courteous to your fellow traveler. Nobody wants to sit next to a "jerk-brain" for three hours.

Enough whining about how to act. You are going to be nice and courteous—I know this because you bought my book. You are calm, intelligent, insightful, and curious, not to mention incredibly good looking. You know how to act because your parents taught you to respect others. Just watch out for the "one percenters." Remember: Some people are never going to change so when we encounter these people while traveling, we simply need to ignore them. If no one has changed them in all their years, you are not going to change them in a two-hour flight. If they persist in bugging you, notify a Flight Attendant. Failure to comply with Flight Attendant safety requests is reason to be tossed off the flight, even at an en route stop. Avoid the tendency to be drawn into juvenile behavior. This temporary lapse of judgment may contribute to a downward spiral of forsaken social mores that ultimately results in a food fight, or other pandemonium in the cabin. This will get you a grip and grin session with the local constabulary upon landing. Let the "one percenter" make an idiot of himself. Ignore him, but don't encourage him.

If you have a concern or a complaint, do feel free to bring it to the attention of the airline. At my company we know that without you, we are "toast." No passengers = No job. We specialize in trying to make your trip trouble free but, if you think we could do something better, please let us know.

> *Security note: After September 11th, we have seen the value of quick-acting observant passengers. The "one percenters" I am describing generally don't present a real security threat. Be ever vigilant of what is going on around you. Feel free to bring any unusual activity to the attention of the Flight Attendants. Quick action by wary passengers has saved several fights in the year since the terrorist attack. More about security in Chapter 10.*

# Get There Early

How many people do you know that just cannot arrive on time to save their souls? For some people, their funeral will be the first occasion they show up on time. I am the opposite. I always try to get there with plenty of spare time.

With the need for tighter security, getting to the airport at least an hour early or more is a must. Two formidable hurdles await the passenger: Check in at the ticket counter and the line through security. How much time you will need at your airport is a function of how busy it is. You may get by with an hour prior to departure at Florence, South Carolina but LAX may require nearly two hours prior to departure, depending on security threats. Check with your airline. It is far better to sit waiting for your departure than it is to wait in line at the ticket counter trying to book a later flight—if one is even available. Besides, getting to an airport early is good because you check in with shorter lines, do important things like go to the bathroom before boarding, and maybe grab a bagel. Also, you may find you can catch the flight right before yours because yours is canceled. "Say WHAT?"

I once had a situation where due to a massive weather system moving in on the airport, it was obvious that my next flight to Las Vegas was going to be greatly delayed or canceled. Knowing what was about to happen, because I had just been glued to the weather radar as I landed, I ran into the terminal to call airline dispatch, only to find that the adjacent gate was boarding a flight to Las Vegas scheduled only 30 minutes before my departure. I called the customer service folks and asked if the thirty or so folks that were early for my flight could get on this earlier flight and get out of town before the storm hit. Customer service checked, and because of the imminent storm, they would accommodate everyone who was there. These passengers, who arrived at the airport and checked in a little early, lucked out. Those who showed up right before departure got a major delay. Once again, the early bird got the worm.

Having related that example, I must now tell you that unless the circumstances are unique, depending on your ticket restrictions, you may be asked to pay a hefty surcharge to change to an earlier flight on my airline and most others. In the above example, due to bookings the airline was able to accommodate my passengers on the earlier flight. But, you never know. It doesn't hurts to ask. Sometimes, in the case of an aircraft maintenance cancellation (when a jet is broken and taken out of service, often referred to as a "mechanical"), the airline may try to accommodate early passengers on an earlier flight if one is available.

## "What do you mean I have to check this?"

First off, the people at the luggage store who sold you your bag lied to you. Even if the suitcase you bought fits in the sizing box that measures the maximum size allowable for carry-ons by most airlines, not *all* carry-ons will fit on the plane. In fact, only about 48 wheeled bags will fill up nearly all the overhead space on an older model 737. Most 737's seat around 130 passengers. That means 82 passengers get to check their carry-on bags too big to fit under the seat. Smaller items will fit under the seats, but the amount of carry-on room is very limited. Not everything that fits in the sizing box will qualify as carry-on baggage. Most airlines limit carry-ons to two items only, not counting purses, coats, etc. Security needs may dictate even less than two items. Furthermore, sizing boxes vary by type and model of aircraft. My crew bag that easily fits in a 737 overhead bin was too large for the sizing box for the L-1011 I flew on to Hawaii. The overhead bins on this jumbo jet are much smaller than those on a 737.

As a general rule, put your lighter items in the overhead bins saving the under-seat area for the heavier items. Remember that the area around your feet must be completely clear. If the item is too big it will have to go in the overhead bin, or be checked. Only very small roller bags will fit under seats and not obstruct aisle access.

The logic is simply to keep the heavier things on the floor; however, heavier items usually are bigger things so that invariably means they get placed overhead. The first concern is that the overhead bins not get overloaded in the event of an accident; you want the overhead bins to stay where they are and not fall on you. Secondly, even after a smooth flight, baggage shifts around in the bins and inevitably someone will get bonked on the head as another passenger hurriedly opens the bin upon arrival at the gate. Simple rule: If it is a really heavy item, check it before flight. Most airlines take the viewpoint that carry-ons are a privilege, not a right and the amount of carry-ons boarded depends solely on how much room is available for storage. If you pre-board due to an injury or other physical condition that precludes you from placing your bag in the overhead bin, the crews at most airlines will go out of their way to help you store your luggage. Relying on Flight Attendants to place bags for even half of the passengers during boarding really becomes impractical, if not impossible. Do you really expect the Flight Attendant to lift 30 or more 50-pound bags into the overhead bin over three or four flights a day? This doesn't even address the problem a Flight Attendant poses to the orderly flow of people trying to board and find their seat, as he or she has to move up and down the aisle hefting bags. Carry-on means just that; you carry your item on, store the item, retrieve the item, and carry the item off the aircraft. If this is out of the question then by all means, check the bag before boarding.

Plan on the possibility of having to check some items in any event. If you are near the end of the boarding group on a full flight and either the Operations Agent boarding the flight, or the Flight Attendant on board asks for your bag, accept their baggage tag receipt and plan to meet your bag in baggage claim at your destination. If the prospect of having to do this is unacceptable, arrive at the airport so you can board in the first boarding group and get your belongings on first. If your airline uses reserved seating, they usually board from the rear of the plane forward so you may have to reserve a seat in the back half of the plane to ensure you have some overhead space for your luggage. Boarding is done by blocks of seat rows so, plan to be among the first in your boarding block. If the airline boards for open seating, getting there early (at least 60 minutes prior to departure) will help get you an early boarding card.

Nonetheless, be forewarned! If your bag is bigger than the sizing box the bag will get snagged, tagged, and sent downstairs faster then you can say, "Huh?" The airlines are very serious about checking bags that are over the size limit. Leave the refrigerator-sized wheel bags at home or check them well in advance.

## "I was the first one to board and there were people already there!"

Don't forget, unless the plane is an originator, the plane that stops at your airport to pick you up probably came from elsewhere. The aircraft may have folks aboard headed to the same place as you, or beyond.

# Delays and Cancellations

On the list of chilling statements to hear when flying, right below "Ladies and gentlemen, if anyone can tell if the wings are still attached, please ring your call button…" is any announcement containing your flight number and the word "CANCELED." The facial expressions of the passengers often remind me of what the Titanic passengers looked like when they were informed there weren't enough lifeboats for everybody. Hey, I've been there as a passenger and believe me, the experience is *no* fun. Some background as to "why" this occurs might help explain this inconvenience.

Despite what you may have heard, airlines are not allowed to cancel flights just because not enough people bought tickets. To my airline's way of thinking, customer service is the reason passengers keep coming back. If we, corporately or individually as employees, run passengers off to other airlines, we will all be unemployed in short order. Canceling or delaying a flight is not a decision made lightly and requires coordination with many groups within the company before a decision is made.

Sometimes, upon landing at an intermediate stop, passengers will be informed by a well-meaning operations person that, "the continuation of this flight has been canceled due to maintenance problems with the plane." Many passengers put two and two together and say, "Hey, wait a minute here! THIS is the plane that is supposed to fly us to our destination—is it broken?" To which the Flight Attendants or operations person says, "Well, no…" What's up with that?

The operations person didn't relay all the details due to time constraints or rapidly changing events behind the scenes. Your aircraft has been chosen to substitute for another plane, which *is* broken. The plane you will ride on will arrive as another later scheduled flight to the broken aircraft's destination. Or perhaps your plane is coming in from another city that will be rerouted onto your canceled flights itinerary. Why do they do that?

This decision is an attempt to inconvenience the least number of passengers. Let's say a full flight suffers equipment problems (airline mumbo-jumbo for a "broken" jet) and another plane is passing through with 35 people going to let's say, Knobnoster. Looking at the flight schedule, there happens to be another flight to Knobnoster only an hour after the earlier flight. If there is room to accommodate all the passengers on that later flight, the airline will "steal" the earlier Knobnoster jet and use that aircraft to get the full flight (whose jet is broken) in the air. The Knobnoster passengers originally scheduled for the earlier Knobnoster flight will then fly on the later scheduled Knobnoster flight.

This whole customer care issue takes careful coordination by airline customer service, maintenance, and airline scheduling personnel. The aim of the whole effort is to minimize the hassle to our customers. If we can make a few passengers 30 minutes late, but still get everyone to their destinations, that is much better than stranding a large number of passengers overnight.

Occasionally, you might encounter an "airplane swap" on a flight that was not supposed to have any plane changes. This is the way a plane can be routed back to a maintenance base for repairs, some required inspections, or to get the aircraft back out to its regular route location after repairs are done. These changes don't usually delay you much other than the inconvenience of having to collect your nest and drag your belongings to another aircraft.

# Following the Rules: "You want me to do what?"

Nothing leaves a bad taste in your mouth like being treated like a child. Like the safety briefings—Who in the heck hasn't been in a car in the last four decades and needs instruction on how to fasten and unfasten your dadgum seatbelt?

In fact, most of the rules we have to enforce are federally mandated, usually by the FAA. Often times, rules have to be written for the "least common denominator" in society. On the surface, the rules seem just plain weird, but if you know some of the reasoning behind them, they make a whole lot more sense. Some common examples:

## Seat Belts

The most basic rule is to keep your seat belt fastened at all times when seated. This seems simple enough but invariably every year a handful of media stories chronicle injuries suffered after turbulence incidents. Often these stories detail serious or fatal injuries that resulted from passengers being thrown around the cabin, usually into the ceiling. Imagine being suspended by your feet over the floor, and without notice being dropped on your head. This is very close to what happens to unsecured passengers, who strike the ceiling because they were not strapped to their seats.

All these injuries could have been avoided if only the people kept their seatbelts at least loosely fastened while seated. Turbulence often arrives unannounced, even on a clear day that was smooth as glass just a second before. Often, you have no time to strap yourself in after the first indication that bumps lie ahead. Turbulence is a non-event with no real impact on safety, except for those needlessly

123

thrown around the cabin. Hey, the pilots *always* stay strapped in. Furthermore, if I am seated in the passenger cabin I don't want some macho "jughead bubba," the size of a linebacker doing a Peter Pan and landing on me. Remember, that seat you're sitting in is bolted to a plane slicing through the air at 500 miles per hour. Sometimes the invisible road ahead is a tad bumpy. Be prepared.

If you see the Flight Attendants up, and moving about, your movement is still restricted by the FASTEN SEAT BELT sign. The pilots may have the sign on because the plane is about to enter an area of known or expected bumpiness, even though the ride is as smooth as a baby's bottom now. By the time you're halfway up that aisle, the ride may get "as rough as a stucco bathtub," as one of our famous Captains used to say. Plus, Flight Attendants have special magnetic shoes that allow them to move safely about the cabin. (Just kidding!) Flight Attendants are very brave individuals who routinely take risks moving about the cabin tending to their beloved passengers. Every year, several are seriously injured due to sudden turbulence. This is why I always seat my Flight Attendants at even the hint of bumps ahead. If your Flight Attendants are seated for turbulence your Captain should have made an announcement, so don't ring your call button. They are restricted from moving around the cabin for their safety and yours.

## Technical Stuff:

*Actually, seatbelts are not required or installed in every car in every country around the world. The FAA wants foreign visitors to be able to unbuckle their seatbelts should the need arise.*

## Tray Tables

Before take-off and landing, passengers are advised to raise their tray tables "to the up and locked position." Part of the reason is to annoy you while you read, or get business done on the incredibly small workspace that is a tray table. The main reason is that a tray table, in the down position, in an aisle seat, blocks that entire row from an unobstructed and smooth evacuation to the aisle. For the same reason, Flight Attendants are very keen to check out that aquarium in a duffel bag you stuffed under the seat in front of you. Any item that sticks into the aisle or seat row may pose a threat to someone trying to get past. Literally seconds can determine the difference between success or failure in a ground evacuation, when smoke or fire is present. Tripping over an item protruding from a seat bottom during a real evacuation is disastrous because inevitably someone will get trampled. The area around your feet *must* be clear.

## Car Seats

The same logic applies to infant seats. Most airlines require that they be placed in a window seat, so that if the need should arise, the mother's delay in unstrapping her infant doesn't delay other passengers from evacuating. Also, they may block egress after an impact if placed in an aisle seat because the seatbacks are designed to "break over" forward like a folding automobile seat in a two-door car, and the car seat may present an obstacle to passengers trying to evacuate.

Infant seating is an understandably tough subject. You can sit in the seat and hold the child on your lap, but in an impact or turbulence situation, the child may not be restrained well enough simply by your holding on. Often, the first instinct of a person beginning to float in the air is to grab at something. In doing so, they inadvertently let go of whatever they have in their hands. You might ask, "Why does the FAA allow children to fly on their parents laps?" The FAA feels that if the parents were denied the option of carrying the child on their laps, some would be forced to drive, and the risk associated with driving is much higher than flying. This thinking may be about to change though.

At this writing, a Notice of Proposed Rulemaking (NPRM) is expected which may end debate once and for all. The FAA may require all passengers to occupy a seat during critical phases of flight which means seats will have to be purchased for every child on every flight. If this proposed rule becomes law, infants will have to be seated in FAA approved car seats during take-off, descent and landing. Check with your airline when making reservations if you have any young ones flying with you. Current regulations require *any* passenger over the age of two to occupy his or her own seat during take-off and landing.

Some people want to put their seatbelt around their child as well as themselves. As in a car, a sudden deceleration would crush the infant or child as the greater body weight of the parent lurched against them. The safest place for your infant child is in an approved rear-facing child seat placed in a forward facing seat, by a window, in a seat you purchased. Currently, some carriers will let you place your child seat in an unoccupied seat for free, but if the plane fills up, you will have to hold the child. The safest solution is to buy a ticket for your child and use an approved car seat. If the proposed FAA rule becomes law, you will not have a choice in the matter. Again, check with your airline regarding the current policy on seating small children.

> *Car Seat Info for Parents: I mentioned the safest seat for an infant or young child is in a rear-facing child seat in a forward facing seat. That may initially sound confusing but this explanation may help.*
>
> *In the early days of commercial aviation, seats were all mounted facing backwards. The reasoning for this was simple; the human body can take tremendous G stresses during a crash situation if seated backwards. During deceleration, the body is already against the seatback and decelerates with the aircraft rather than a forward-facing passenger who continues forward as the aircraft decelerates, eventually striking the seat in front of them. For this reason, a child placed in a rear-facing car seat strapped securely into a forward facing seat is well protected from deceleration impacts. Just remember: Keep your child's back to the impact.*
>
> *Current FAA regulations require that Child Restraint Systems (CRSs), or Child Restraint Devices (CRDs) as they may also be called, be government approved for use on an aircraft. The label*

*should say, "This restraint is certified for use in motor vehicles and aircraft." Furthermore, the FAA recommends that:*

*—children under 20 lbs be placed in a rear facing CRS*

*—children from 20-40 lbs be placed in a forward-facing child restraint*

*—children over 40 lbs use an aircraft seatbelt (no CRS)*

*Booster seats and harness vests may enhance safety in automobiles, but they are banned for use on aircraft. These devices should be checked as baggage. Finally, many airlines offer significant fare discounts to children under the age of two so check with your airline when you make reservations. Some airlines may require a copy of a birth certificate for age verification, so bring a copy along just in case. You wouldn't believe how many people try to pawn off forty-pound five-year-olds as a lap children just to save a few bucks. For the latest FAA safety information check with your airline or visit the FAA site at www.faa.gov or you can call the FAA consumer information hotline at 1-800-322-7873 (1-800-FAA-SURE).*

*Why did rear-facing seats disappear on commercial planes? The public did not like them and this demand led the airlines to install them facing forward, like those in automobiles. The military still places their passenger seats facing rearwards in many of their transport aircraft.*

## Customers of Size

Since we just discussed smaller passengers, its appropriate to touch on folks nearer the other end of the size spectrum. For those who need a little extra room, seatbelt extensions are available and can be obtained from the Flight Attendant during or shortly after boarding. Should you have unique need regarding seating, mention it upon check-in at the airport and accommodations will be made if available. They may allow you to change to a seat that has no adjacent fellow passenger, and this will allow you to relax by folding the armrest back and stretching out in two seats. Passengers of size should understand that this is a service provided solely based on the availability of empty seats on the aircraft. If the flight is full, customers unable to sit in one seat may be asked to purchase two seats. These rules are specified by the Air Carrier Access Act, which all airlines must comply with. (The Americans with Disabilities Act does not apply to aircraft accommodations.) If need be, ask to be preboarded.

For those average sized passengers who find themselves a little cramped by a customer of size seated next to them, mention it to the airline Customer Service Representative when you arrive at your destination and quite often the airline will make accommodations for your inconvenience.

## Storage of Large Items Behind Bulkhead Seats

Often, passengers have a large framed poster/picture or folio case for business use and they want to sit next to a bulkhead seat and slide their item between the seatback and the bulkhead. Initially, this makes perfect sense. The only problem is, in a bumpy landing or crash situation where evacuation is necessary, this large item will almost assuredly be launched free of its hiding place, and block the aisle. This is a big no-no. Some aircraft are equipped with portfolio cases in the rear of the cabin or closets up front and the Flight Attendants will store the pictures there, if they fit inside. Otherwise, they will have to be checked.

## Balloons

Flight attendants on some airlines will not allow fully inflated kids balloons on board. When I first heard this I was aghast. "No Mickey Mouse? How un-American can that be?" The reasoning is very simple. Filled balloons pop at cruising cabin altitude and the Mylar (silvery) balloons sound *very* loud. Remember: Higher altitude=lower cabin pressure. Some Flight Attendants will allow the balloons if slightly deflated and will warn passengers seated around the overhead bin that they may hear a muffled pop should the balloon burst inflight.

## Stupid Unrelated Balloon Stories

When I was a kid in Chicago, they handed out silver Mylar balloons to the first 5,000 people who entered Wrigley Field for a baseball game. The plan was that at a special point during the game, everyone would release his or her balloon en masse. The idea seemed really cool until all these balloons floated way up into O'Hare airspace, where they jammed the ATC approach radar. The silvery mylar reflected the radar signal making the balloons appear on radar as one giant aircraft. O' Hare took something like two to three hour delays until the balloons all blew away from the city The military uses this same technique to confuse enemy radar and they call it "chaff."

More Mickey Mouse trivia: Mylar balloons will occasionally float up above 30,000 feet without popping. Once over Las Vegas I saw a silvery object headed right towards my plane that, at first looked for all the world, like another plane. In the two to three seconds I had to react, I saw the unmistakable outline of those familiar mouse ears. In a split second, Mickey Mouse's smiling face shot by about 30 feet right off our right wing tip. We were so close I could actually make out the string tied under the balloon. Mickey wouldn't have hurt the plane had we hit him, but the sight of a silvery object closing on my aircraft at 400 miles per hour sure got my attention. "Brain to body—Ignore the adrenaline….This was only a test."

## Electronic Devices

Today, hardly anyone leaves home without some kind of electric "doo-dad." From cell phones to GameBoys® to laptop computers to personal stereos, each offers great utility and pleasure to the operator, as well as a host of safety related issues to the flight crew. By all means, bring them along, but please use them in accordance with crew suggestion and FAA regulation.

## Cell Phones

I bet today, at least one-half to three-quarters of the traveling public is carrying a phone with them. I know virtually every crew-member has one. While they make life really easy for the user, they can occasionally make life really tough for the pilot.

Once, on approach to Burbank Airport in California, I was unable to contact the tower for clearance to land. The tower controller could hear us asking for landing clearance, but we were unable to hear him clearing us to land. A Flight Attendant called and reported that there was a young teenage boy on his cell phone who would not turn it off despite pleading by the Flight Attendants. We realized the connection with our radio problem and advised her to, "Get the danged thing away from him and turn it off...NOW!" In a second, our communications with the tower was restored, we were cleared to land, and the story ended happily. Apparently, the kid's cell phone signal was louder to our radio than the tower controller's radio signal. All this transpired in about two minutes. A call by a kid to his girlfriend to come pick him up at the airport seemed like a good idea at the time, at least to him.

*Never* use cell phones inflight or any time the front entry door is closed, regardless of what the media or your cell phone salesperson tells you. Remember, you are in a metal box and the signal may interfere with the pilot's radio communications. Use the seatback phones if provided. They are designed for use anytime.

## Laptop Computers

Did you know your laptop is a radio station? Indeed, and a powerful one at times. Ever notice the "CLASS B COMPUTING DEVICE" warning stickers on the bottom of devices with microprocessors, advising you to move the device farther away if it interferes with another electronic device?

Part of the technical reason behind the limitations we are now experiencing with PC clock speeds is that the frequencies generated by computers are powerful, and circuits radiating their frequencies to another circuit board within the computer create problems. Some of this "noise" escapes the box and may interfere with other electronic devices. Not a good thing, especially if the pilot is flying an approach in bad weather to minimums. As you polish off that letter on your laptop some of your stray signals might interfere with the signal "beam" the pilot is flying to the runway. Even in nice weather, pilots are sometimes on very narrow approach paths and need their navigation signals uninterrupted. Think about this: Hundreds of new electronic products come out every year and nobody tests these things inside an aircraft for possible interference. Interference problems are rare, but at least up at cruise altitude, should a problem occur, it is apt to be a minor one.

Minor that is, for non fly-by-wire aircraft. Newer aircraft, where all flight controls are operated by electronic signal with little or no cable back up, are called fly-by-wire and present a different problem. Wiring that carries the signals to the flight controls runs through the fuselage. I have heard from friends within the industry that, as these aircraft systems experience incidents where laptops are believed to be the culprit, portable computers may ultimately and understandably be banned from use during flight on these aircraft. Period. For the record, the Boeing 737 is not one of the planes affected. Neither are Boeing's 727, 747, 757, 767, and MD-80/90/95 series aircraft. Lockheed's L-1011 is old technology and similarly not affected. Still though, turning off laptops in any aircraft during take-off and landing makes good sense.

## Personal Stereos

Once, I was seated behind the emergency exit row. During the pre-take-off cabin inspection, a Flight Attendant stopped by the emergency exit row and told a teenage boy to remove his headphones during take-off and landing. On a subsequent pass through the cabin, just prior to take-off, the Flight Attendant again noticed the boy was still wearing his headphones and requested he remove them. The boy's mother was seated ahead of me. I saw the look of consternation and annoyance at the Flight Attendant's request. "What harm can this cause?" the mother asked those passengers seated around her.

"A bunch," I advised. "It assures your son won't be trampled to death if the Captain decides it's necessary to stop the take-off and begin an emergency evacuation. Your son, deep into his new *Nine Inch Nails* CD may not notice what's going on as a result of the 99 decibel tunage blasting between his ears. Your child, oblivious to the Flight Attendants command to evacuate, say out the rear of the aircraft, steps into the aisle as he sees everyone else standing up, and he gets trampled. All because he was unable to hear the Flight Attendants commands. Plus, how is he supposed to hear the pre-departure safety briefing?" Faced with the common sense reasoning behind the request—the mother quipped to her son, "Get those things off your head!" I know the boy never heard my reasoning; hopefully mom explained to him later. Headphones are fine in flight but take them off during take-off and landing.

Another reason radios must be turned off has to do with the same radio frequency radiation as laptops. If you are jamming to 108 FM on your Walkman® radio, you are actually broadcasting on 108 FM as well. 108 FM happens to be a navigation frequency used by planes. Radios operate by sticking a voice signal, or in this case a music signal, to a constant frequency carrier signal and that combination is broadcast into the air. At the receiving end, the tuner synthesizes the carrier frequency, say 108mhz FM, and that frequency is stripped away from the radio signal leaving the voice or music we listen to. That synthesized frequency can leak out of the radio, and on occasions, can interfere with navigation equipment.

A friend of mine in the Air Force was done with his turn at the controls on a training flight and went back to listen to the ball game on his AM radio. As he tuned through the radio spectrum and found the game, he noticed whenever he turned his radio on, the plane turned. Puzzled, he switched off the game and the plane straightened out. Turning the game on again, the plane turned. Wondering what was up, he went to the cockpit where they were having a discussion about the signal from a ground based navigation aid. One minute the needle on the dashboard would point to the navigation aid on the ground several miles in front of the aircraft, the next minute it was trying to point at my friend's radio in the back of the airplane. The reason: Both the navaid and the Walkman were transmitting on nearly the same AM frequency. The Walkman just happened to be closer to the antenna so the signal it sent out was stronger than the navaid many miles away.

# Deplaning

A threat to disembarking passengers is small children waiting in the jetway with their parents for car seats or strollers to be brought up from the baggage bins. Most parents are mindful of the deplaning passengers but, some parents let their kids wander in the jetway. I watched a businessman in Texas walk off the plane in a hurry only to broadside a two year old child with his briefcase who was playing in the area around the forward exit door. The businessman couldn't have expected a small child to dart out from behind the entry door and fortunately the child wasn't seriously injured. Be mindful of children who have mindless parents.

A note about carry-ons: The small wheel bags that are all the rage are wonderful items. I use one myself. A problem often results when, upon leaving the aircraft, some people stop right in the middle of the narrow jetway to put their bag down, pull the handle up, and, on occasion, hang another bag on the wheel bag before continuing on their way. This totally blocks the flow off the airplane. If these passengers would simply step to the side of the jetway or carry their bags up the jetway and assemble them inside the terminal, nobody would be delayed. Be careful following someone out of the aircraft carrying a wheel bag. They may stop suddenly as they exit the aircraft.

We've covered some of the rules we impose on you while you are within our care. Some of them seem "hokey" or "dumb," but if you have a question about a subject we didn't cover, catch a Flight Attendant after the rest of the passengers get served and ask them, they'll be glad to explain the reasoning behind a rule. If that is not possible, just do your best to comply with a request from a crewmember, and rest assured, we really don't make these rules up to inconvenience you. Flight crews will use as much latitude as they can, but the FAA rules regarding passenger seating and baggage stowage are very clear and leave little room for interpretation. Again, the rule usually comes down to a safety issue.

Okay. We have nailed down all the "inside the airplane" stuff. Now, how about that darkening sky out the window?

In the next chapter, let's look at Aviation Weather.

*From the first line of a seatback emergency information card:*

*"Please contact a USAir Express crewmember if you are not able to read, speak, or understand English, or are unable to understand the graphic directions or crew commands."*

# Eight:

# Aviation Weather

**As** someone who works in the sky nearly every day, I have a special insight into the workings of weather. I have garnered a healthy respect for the power of Mother Nature and I constantly marvel at the subtleties and dramatic differences that occur within a short time or distance.

Walking up my driveway in Arizona early one spring morning I was awestruck by a gorgeous pre-sunrise twilight. The wind on the ground was blowing at a gusty 20-30 miles per hour as I tried to gather up my newspaper. Above me at 35,000 feet was a solitary jet, headed towards Los Angeles. The contrail off the jet was brilliant white against the deep blue twilight sky, and spread back towards the horizon in a perfectly straight line, undisturbed by any winds at altitude. Usually, conditions are just the opposite.

On the ground the winds can be dead calm and yet only five miles straight up, a jet stream core of fast moving air can be blowing at 120 miles per hour. At my house in late June the temperature can be 110 degrees, but only five miles straight up the temperature can be 40 below zero. Think of that next time you fly; forty below zero on the other side of the little Plexiglas window. This thing we call the atmosphere, which seems larger than the whole planet, is actually like the skin on an apple; a very thin layer that surrounds the earth.

We are only now beginning to understand how all the interconnected aspects of weather affect one another. Why do weather patterns in Africa produce hurricanes in the Atlantic waters off Florida? Why do fast moving layers of air approaching each other at right angles create a rotor of wind that suddenly turns 90 degrees and forms what we call a tornado? This stuff is way beyond me. As a pilot, I just want to see the weather problems ahead and avoid them. I have been asked many times what actually constitutes bad weather, and after some thought, the following pretty much sums up my view:

> *Nutshell Definition: "Bad weather" for aviation is any weather phenomenon that exceeds the climb capability of an airplane at a low altitude (landing or take-off) and forces it to fly into the ground. Or, any phenomenon that causes the airplane to be buffeted with hail or winds, resulting in loss of controllability of the aircraft, causing damage to the aircraft structure or any passengers and crew not seated with their seatbelts fastened.*

That weather has played a factor in airline accidents in the past is common knowledge. What many people do not know is that a good number of the accidents initially identified as "weather related," were in fact, breakdowns in leadership or crew coordination. Basically, perfectly good airplanes were allowed to fly into hazardous weather the pilots knew might exist. The pilots simply failed to realize how dangerous the weather was or believed they could withstand the weather conditions. In many cases, the airplane was quite capable of flying out of the predicament but, for reasons largely due to training standards at the time, the crew failed to maximize the performance capabilities of the aircraft. The unfortunate result: Catastrophe.

In the aftermath of these accidents crew training has emphasized two distinct but related areas: Crew Resource Management—how the crew works together and Weather Recognition and Avoidance—how to recognize bad weather and how to deal with what lies ahead.

Weather recognition is pretty simple to teach. Modern simulators will shake your fillings out during a windshear approach. Once pilots know what to look for in terms of radar returns, weather reports, and other information, they become keenly aware of those danger signals. After experiencing the violence of an encounter in the simulator, the message is hardwired into the pilot's brain: Be aware of what may lie ahead, and if confirmed, perform the escape maneuver immediately. I know because I've encountered severe turbulence low to the ground a few times, and the training I've received made me distinctly aware of the risks associated with continuing the approach. We high-tailed it out of that area and landed elsewhere. Before I get you all concerned, we'll examine different types of "bad weather." First though, a quick look at where pilots get their weather information.

A lady passenger told me she watches the Weather Channel for about a week before she flies because weather is her biggest concern. I watch the Weather Channel too, but only for general information. What weather systems are near my intended route, will a coat be needed, will it be wet, etc. The media once made the statement that passengers have better access to weather information than pilots do. Not at *my* airline. The information relayed in my airline weather packet is very detailed and specific. I get a radar summary of what the USA looks like in terms of weather radar returns. These radar returns identify thunderstorms, their associated high winds, and other potential problems. I also get last-hour observations for every destination my company serves as well as alternate airports, if necessary, telling me the winds, visibility, temperature, and cloud layers. In addition, I get forecasts for applicable cities along my route of flight. If I think there is a need for a more up-to-date picture, I go call "Mother" (company dispatch). The Dispatcher that is handling my flight can pull up real-time weather radar anywhere along my route of flight, and tell me exactly what is happening. I can even call Mother on the radio en route and ask for updates or have them sent to me electronically. Dispatch can see an overlay on their radar representing the aircraft flying in a sector and give me hints as to which way those ahead of me are going around weather. If weather at the destination has gone goofy, my Dispatcher and I can decide to go elsewhere and wait the weather out. Mother's whole reason for existence is to stay current on weather and field conditions that might affect his/her/my flight. Every airliner in the skies has another set of eyes on the ground watching out for problems ahead. Dispatchers do a very important job.

Some of the best information comes from other aircraft ahead of us. "Ride reports" or other information can be passed over ATC radio frequencies, and if somebody encounters something unusual, most sing out for any aircraft that may be following through the same area. Professional courtesy, backed up by Federal Aviation Regulation demands immediate notification to ATC if anything extraordinary is encountered, so that warnings can be issued to other planes in the area. This is largely why you often see the "Fasten Seatbelt" sign illuminated for longer periods on the first flight of the day: Because most late-night passenger jets land before dawn, the pilots have no one ahead to check rides with and expect the possibility of turbulence. Also, later in the day, ride reports ahead may indicate bumps ahead even though it is currently smooth. In this case the Captain will keep the passengers seated expecting the ride to deteriorate.

So, we have all this information available, what is important?

Flying a plane full of passengers thousands of miles through occasional stormy weather is a very complex task. I liken the challenge to cracking a diamond: Much preparation followed by professional execution. Do the task incorrectly and you are left with nothing. Choose wisely and correctly and the result is a joy to behold, at least for the pilots. The passengers seated in the cabin may have never noticed the weather outside.

## Dark Skies Ahead—What Really Is Bad Weather?

Not to make the discussion any more complex, but what constitutes "bad weather" is all relative. The worst thunderstorm you can imagine along my route of flight is no big deal if I can simply fly around the stormy area. Thunderstorms only present a problem if you fly through one or get caught in a nasty wind underneath one, especially during take-off or landing. You can see rainstorms with radar, or your eyes; one peek is worth a thousand radar sweeps as we like to say, and depending on what stage of growth they are at and how big they've grown, they might be like sleeping grizzlies; they may eat you, but not right now. For the present, it is safe to pass the sleeping giant. Let's examine the threat thunderstorms pose.

## Thunderstorms—Rain Clouds On Steroids

Stay with me now, this is really simple stuff wrapped in some big words.

Clouds are visible moisture. Moisture is all around us and though we can feel it as humidity, usually we can't *see* it. Moisture gets lifted due to convection: Warm air, like the heat off a candle flame, rising into cooler air that keeps it rising even more. As this moist air gets lifted by warmer air into the cooler air, at some point the moisture becomes visible, like fog. A creature called the "dewpoint" is where the air of a given humidity will form visible moisture at a certain temperature and we call this the "dewpoint temperature." Real simple stuff: Chill moisture laden air and *voila*, fog forms; like out of the air conditioning vent in planes, on the ground in humid areas, or out of a freezer in a garage in the summer months. Ground fog is just a cloud on the ground. Clouds are globs of fog in the sky. See? I told you this stuff was simple.

Clouds present NO problem to a pilot except during take-off and landing, in that you have to be able to see the runway to do both. Can't see the runway suitably for take-off? Sorry, can't go. Can't see the runway at the end of your approach? Sorry, you will have to go around and either try again or go land somewhere else. We have instruments that will allow us to land and take-off in near "pea-soup" fog, but we still have to be able to see a little bit of the runway.

Ice forms in some clouds at the freezing level but ice is NOT a big concern to large airliners, especially at cruise altitude where it is usually too cold for ice to form. (Later in this chapter we will look at how icing affects operations in more detail.)

## Thunderstorms: The Building Phase

Big clouds become rain showers and they pose little threat to an airliner. You will often experience a bumpy ride due to the air currents swirling around inside a rain cloud, but remember, you are zooming along at hundreds of miles per hour. You know what a 30 mph gust does to your car on the freeway. In a plane you do not have to stay in narrow traffic lanes, so the effect is not as critical.

If the air is unstable and lifting forces are great, some clouds become thunderstorms. If rain showers are teddy bears, thunderstorms are grizzlies. The winds inside a thunderstorm can exceed 100 miles per hour, and believe-you-me, pilots know this and will avoid them at all costs. Pilots may even intentionally disregard headings or altitude changes given by ATC if they place the aircraft in the vicinity of a storm. If need be, the Captain can exercise his emergency authority, authorizing him to maneuver his plane as necessary, to remain clear of the weather. Even skirting around the edges will often produce a rough ride. Sometime this is unavoidable, as thunderstorms tend to line up in strings of several in a row. Oddly enough, we call this a "line" of thunderstorms. Often, the only way around a line is to fly hundreds of miles out of the way, across the next state if necessary. You can't fly above the big storms. In the summer, they exceed 50,000 feet, which is above the capability of most airliners.

A large thunderstorm is a melding of God's majesty and Mother Nature's incredible power. When conditions are just right, almost always a summer phenomenon, a rainstorm with a core of warm rising air begins building faster and faster. As literally thousands upon thousands of tons of moisture rise up through the freezing level, the characteristic frosty "mushroom head" shape forms. Sometimes these white clouds almost explode vertically, often exceeding the climb capability of jet aircraft. During this "building" phase, the storm is sucking up moisture from its base, and if you were standing on the ground facing the storm, the wind would be at your back. Picture Mother Nature's own giant Hoover vacuum, and you have the right idea (see Figure 25).

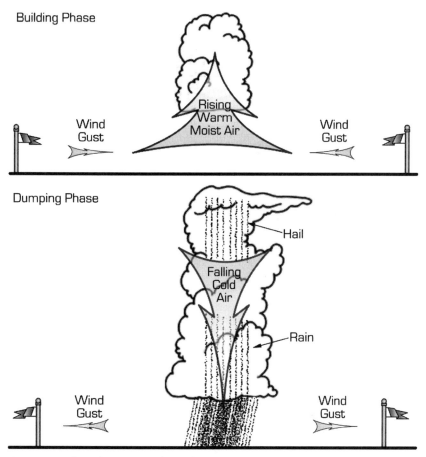

*Figure 25. Thunderstorm Life Cycle*

Sometimes upper level jet-stream winds will have ripped the top of the thunderstorm off, scattering the frosty upper layers for many miles, giving the storm that really menacing look. During the building phase these storms are fairly benign, and as long as you stay out of them, they are much like a sleeping grizzly: You can tip-toe around the edge at lower altitudes without feeling its presence, but in literally seconds, conditions can change drastically.

## The Dumping Phase

At some point the weight of the moisture lifted will equal the motive force that lifted the water high above ground, and the whole grand Sno-Cone machine will grind to a halt. Slowly the frozen water hefted some five to ten miles up into the atmosphere will start to fall, and the whole process reverses. This usually happens late in the day, as the sun gets low on the horizon. Remember, the sun is the power source that runs the world's weather. When the sun folds up shop at days end, the power to build the storms is diminished. That is why you see very few thunderstorms at sunrise, and is yet another reason I fly mornings. If you were facing the storm at this point in time, the wind at your back would stop for a minute or two, and then suddenly become a blast of cold air in your face.

As the thunderstorm begins to dump moisture, the water half-way up this "escalator into space," will turn around and fall as rain. Very quickly the rain will intensify in a very tight core or rain shaft. This downward movement of moisture drags the air with it, producing the "gust front," or "first gust," as it spreads out from the base of the storm. This is what produces the tell-tale dust storm on the ground. This falling shaft of air produces what is often referred to as a "wind shear," or in very extreme cases a "microburst." During the mid-Seventies we began to identify this phenomenon. Now, with ground based Doppler weather radar, we can see moving rain in these intense shafts at the core of a thunderstorm.

Finally, the shaft of falling air has accelerated to an extremely high velocity, often in excess of 100 miles per hour, straight down. The ice from up high doesn't have time to melt as it falls, and the rain that was falling a second before turns to hail balls. Mother Nature has opened up the freezers of near-space and let that cold air fall like a freight train, propelled by the weight of thousands of tons of water. When I hear of, or see first gust, I get out of the way. When I hear reports of hail, I get out of town. A battle with Mother Nature over arrival times is unwinnable at this point.

In review, thunderstorms pose different threats at different times of their lives. Pilots basically avoid them at all costs, and are keenly interested in where they are and what they are doing when it comes time to take-off or land. Their size varies and the affected area may be only a few square miles—or a few hundred square miles. Training emphasizes clues to problems that may lie ahead, and pilots practice windshear escape maneuvers every time they train in the simulator. Let me further explain a windshear.

Before I started flying, I naturally assumed that the wind I felt on the ground was the same wind that was everywhere above me, all blowing the same direction. The atmosphere is not that simple. On the ground, you might feel the wind blowing from the north at 10 mph, and only 1,000 feet above you the wind can be blowing 20 mph from the south. The sky is a fluid mass of changing air currents, like a stream with eddies and currents around the edges. That mix of airflows is what allows people to fly hot air balloons on cross country races—they change directions by climbing into a layer of air going the direction the pilot wants to go.

A windshear is that boundary area between two masses of air going different directions. They occur at all times of the day in all types of weather, and passengers usually notice them as a bump or two as they fly along. An airliner may pass through a hundred areas of changing wind direction in the course of a normal flight, most gradual and not that noticeable from the cabin. Turbulence is produced by these changing eddies of air and presents no problem as long as everyone is strapped into their seats.

*Safety Note: Once again, the plane is built to handle this turbulence, but people who aren't strapped in and get tossed around the cabin often end up getting injured. This is why it's absolutely essential that if you don't need to be up and moving around the cabin, ALWAYS keep your seatbelt on, even loosely, just in case the plane enters an unforeseen area of bumps. Passengers have been severely injured, or even killed as a result of injuries sustained from being thrown about the cabin. These injuries could*

143

> *have been avoided simply by being held in their seat, by their seatbelts. Turbulence is exciting for sure, but nothing to worry about as long as you are buckled in. Your pilots will do everything they can to avoid areas of turbulence but, in some cases, virtually the entire sky in a given region may be choppy and bumpy and there is no other choice than to get through as quickly as possible. Remember: Clear air turbulence is invisible.*

Usually the changing layers of wind are like two sheets of paper laid on a table, each going different directions horizontally (horizontal shear, see Figure 26). The plane encounters these as it climbs up to altitude or descends to land. These occasionally provide a bump or two, but present little threat to the plane. This is why the pilots leave the FASTEN SEAT BELT sign on during climb, just to be safe. The pilot knows the plane is passing through layers of moving air that might provide a bump ahead. Horizontal shears present a problem to pilots during landing in that the plane may suddenly fly into a layer going the same direction as the plane, causing the aircraft to lose airspeed. As long as it's not too much, the pilot can compensate by carrying a few extra knots so that when the shear is passed, they are above minimum approach speed. If the shear presents a headwind, it's no big deal, the plane gets fast for a few seconds, and the pilot slows back to approach speed. Shears of 10-15 mph or more are not uncommon, and are usually reported to landing aircraft by the tower from reports received by previous aircraft. Sometimes these wind phenomena last only a few minutes and then disappear completely.

All is not flat in the world of weather, and horizontal shears can bend down like the tectonic plates of the earth's crust. This happens along frontal boundaries, and means the wind can be moving upward or downward at an angle. As a passenger, this doesn't really mean anything except more potential for bumps.

A thunderstorm in the dumping mode produces that high-speed vertical shaft of falling cold air where the rain and hail is present. This vertical shear is unique in aviation weather, and presents a real danger to the flight in that the air can fall faster than the

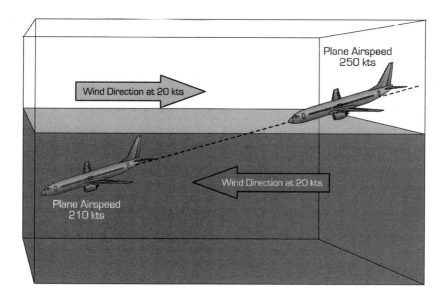

*Figure 26. Windshear*

plane can climb out of it. If the plane is climbing through the air at a vertical speed of 70 miles per hour, and the column of air the plane is in is falling at 100 miles per hour, the plane relative to the ground is descending at 30 miles per hour. The plane's only hope for escape is to quickly climb and maintain that climb long enough to escape the concentrated shaft of falling air. This is what pilots practice in the simulator. Wind shear training is a very effective tool to have in your bag of tricks, but the best plan is to avoid areas of potential major shear activity entirely. (As I said before, "He who scares and runs away, lives to fly another day.")

## The Iceman Cometh

So far we've covered thunderstorms, rain showers and the wind-shears the plane may encounter. What other kinds of weather should we be concerned about? We touched on icing earlier, and I wanted to cover a few more items.

Modern jet aircraft are tested during certification to see how they operate in various magnitudes of icing conditions. The Boeing

737, like all commercial aircraft, has an extremely effective de-ice system for use inflight. Certain planes tend to accumulate ice more than others. The 737, for some reason, does not tend to accumulate much ice. If it does in extreme weather conditions, the de-ice system melts it off the critical wing leading edges, in short order. I have only had to turn this system on a few dozen times in twenty years. In addition, the various sensors and probes on the plane are heated to over 400 degrees Fahrenheit to prevent any ice build-up. Even the cockpit front windows are heated partly to prevent ice from obscuring the pilot's vision (see Figure 27).

Snow usually doesn't stick to the plane inflight. Occasionally, a thin line will form along the leading edge of the wing and is easily seen from the cabin. This presents no problem to the aircraft and will usually melt early in descent well prior to landing. If needed, the pilots can turn on their leading edge anti-ice system and melt off the accumulations using bleed air heat from the engines.

On the ground, ice formation from freezing rain most often starts slowly sticking to objects on the ground so there is usually plenty of warning before it begins to affect flight operations. Freezing rain is one of the biggest enemies of commercial aviation. Warm rain falling into a lower sub-freezing temperature can coat everything with an almost invisible coating of ice. The jet airliner is really only bothered by freezing rain during take-off and landing. Ice in the form of freezing rain can build up so quickly that it can disturb the airflow over the wing and affect the lift produced. With this in mind, the FAA has set limits for the intensity of freezing rain falling at the airport: Exceed these limits, and you are not legal to take-off or land.

Once on the ground, any acquired ice will be removed before the next flight. Icy runways may make taking off or landing impossible, but then airlines won't attempt operations in these conditions. The airports measure braking capability and relay that to pilots. Below a certain braking traction, operations cease. Don't you wish you had that level of information for the roads you drive on? Also, planes are landing every minute or so and are being queried by the control tower about braking conditions. If the braking action on the

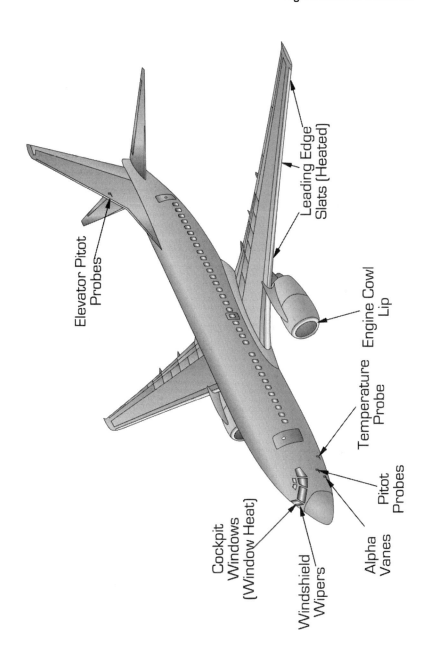

*Figure 27. Anti-Ice Locations*

runway becomes questionable, operations are suspended until the runway can be sanded or cleared. Pilot reports are critical in icing conditions, and everyone is keenly interested in what the last plane to land encountered. Once you are flying, ice is of no real consequence. The plane can shed accumulated ice off the wing at will. Ice accumulated on the tail and fuselage during landing adds a few extra pounds to the aircraft but essentially operations in the mildest of icing conditions is not a problem. Freezing rain poses the biggest problem to planes undergoing de-icing prior to take-off as the rain washes off the de-ice fluid and greatly reduces the time a plane can remain free of ice on the ground. We call the time after de-ice procedures are begun and the latest charted time the plane can expect to have the de-ice fluid still doing the job, the "holdover time." Exceed this holdover time and the aircraft must be de-iced once again if any buildup is visible on exterior surfaces. At anything above light freezing rain, take-off and landing operations cease.

Even though the airplane is capable of handling icing encountered inflight, the best course of action is to avoid moderate or worse icing conditions. At my company the view of management is "If we need aircraft wing de-icing systems on for take-off, should we even be thinking about taking off?" No: We take the conservative route and wait until conditions improve.

*What are "de-ice procedures" and how can we take off with snow still falling?*

On the ground, icing presents a new host of issues. Parked at the gate or taxiing to and from the runway, there is no wind over the plane as occurs in flight, and falling snow and ice can build up quickly on the aircraft. Even light snow can stick to the warmer parts of the plane as it sits at the gate. This partially melted slush can refreeze into a thick, rough layer that destroys lift on the wing and control surfaces of the plane. Before you take off you want a clean smooth surface on the wings and tail as well as a clean fuselage. That is where deice procedures come into play.

Years ago, planes were sprayed before leaving the gate. The fluid used was essentially like warmed anti-freeze similar to that in your car radiator. This worked fine if the gate was a short distance from the runway, and no delay was anticipated before take-off. After one accident, investigators found that, depending on the amount and type of falling precipitation, a plane might be contaminated with ice and snow accretions within only a few minutes of de-ice procedures. This was unacceptable. The FAA and the airlines completely rethought how de-ice procedures should be accomplished, and the new procedure is a vast improvement.

Now planes are de-iced very close to the end of the runway they will depart from. This allows the aircraft to take-off very quickly after de-icing and this ensures the de-icing fluid is still working well. Over time, as de-ice fluid melts ice and snow, it becomes diluted and therefore less effective. Furthermore, the crews doing the actual de-ice procedure are trained in what to look for after applying de-ice fluid, to be sure all contamination is removed from the plane. As yet another safety step, pilots are required to inspect portions of the plane just prior to take-off, to ensure the outside is free of ice or snow. This may include actually walking back into the cabin to take one last look to make sure the wings and control surfaces are clean and clear for take-off. And further yet, pilots can refer to those charted, hold-over times, which identify how long a plane can safely wait before take-off, given the type of fluid applied and the type of weather conditions present at the airport. This new approach to de-icing operations has been very effective.

Some mornings, you may see frost, like that on a car, on a plane in the early morning. Hoarfrost, a thin film crystalline, semi-transparent frost may be left on the wings and fuselage in certain areas and not affect the performance of the aircraft. This thin frost will evaporate shortly after take-off. Hoarfrost usually forms after cold cloudless nights during Spring and Fall.

As in all types of weather operations, the pilot is entrusted not only with the passengers onboard his or her plane but bears some responsibility for those passengers in the planes to follow. I cannot overemphasize the importance of pilot reports to ATC and the other aircraft on frequency. Other pilots are depending on me to sing out if something I encounter isn't safe. I have no reservations about speaking up, whether the concern is weather, turbulence or whatever. During a particularly nasty storm in the San Francisco Bay area, my pilot report of severe turbulence shut down San Francisco, Oakland International and San Jose International for several hours one morning. I was later thanked by a Captain who was about to enter that area, but upon hearing my report to ATC, simply returned to Los Angeles rather than expose his crew and passengers to peril during an attempt to land.

One note about management pressures on pilots to fly in bad weather: No company worth it's salt, would ask a pilot to do something he thought unwise or beyond his capabilities. I have heard horror stories about pilots who worked flying freight or hauling mail for small companies, being strongly encouraged to fly in challenging weather conditions. At my company I have complete freedom and latitude to do *anything* I deem necessary to protect my plane and the passengers, with full company support. My management trusts me to make good decisions based on safety first, passenger comfort second, and schedule third. Period. I have arrived home five hours late because I chose to sit out the weather at the gate until conditions improved. Not a word from my Company about trying to stay on schedule. That is the way flight operations should be conducted.

Again we have tackled a very complex subject. You have now been exposed to more aspects and concerns regarding weather than most beginning private pilots encounter. It's not important that you know all the details, but rather have an overall understanding of what really matters to the safe completion of your flight, and what the airline and flight crew is doing to ensure you arrive safely at your destination. Hopefully, time permitting, your pilots will keep you up to date on the weather ahead and offer some insight as to how they plan to deal with Mother Nature's challenges. With the information discussed in this chapter, you can rest assured; your pilots are weighing all aspects of the situation ahead in order to choose the safest course of action.

As for the "weather" brewing inside your body as you fly along, lets take a look at what effect flying has on the body in Chapter 9, "Aerospace Physiology."

*If knowledge can create problems,*
*it is not through ignorance that we can solve them.*

—Isaac Asimov (1920-1992)

# Nine:

# Aerospace Physiology 101

## "Why Do My Ears Hurt?"

**On** occasion deplaning passengers give me the eye and make some comment about, "how bad the pressurization was on this flight." Invariably they describe some kind of ear or sinus pain that didn't exist before the flight. Most folks who offer this complaint get miffed when I suggest that the problem probably stems from a slight cold or some other subtle illness they probably didn't recognize as they packed for the trip. Truth is, usually this kind of "hidden" cold doesn't add up to much discomfort—until you fly.

Before we discuss details about how the planes pressurization system operates or how your sinuses are supposed to work, let me say that modern pressurization systems are very reliable and very automated. Most aircraft have pressurization systems that have one or two back up systems to "take-over" in case something happens to the computer controlling the pressure within the cabin. In twenty years of flying I have only witnessed two malfunctions, one I described earlier where I was a passenger and experienced a loss of cabin pressure, and one other instance where the cabin pressure controller failed and slowly started letting the air out of the plane. In the latter case, we switched to yet another standby system and continued without further incident. The system is very reliable and very good at controlling the cabin pressure for those in good health. Problems arise when the venting system used to equalize the pressures within our body becomes blocked.

Now, before I go describing evolved gasses, partial pressures and body cavities, let me first remind you that I am not a medical doctor. I am an aircrew member with over two decades of experience in high altitude flight in various types of jet aircraft. I have been trained by the United States Air Force in aerospace physiology, and the effects high speed and high altitude flight have on the human body. This training, along with my flight experience, gives me a unique view into this phenomenon that only a small percentage of passengers understand. Aerospace medicine is a highly specialized aspect of medicine and little of this information is readily available to the general public. I think having this information is critical, for the crewmember and passenger alike, to understand how humans are built, and how pressurized flight affects them. This knowledge is important to prevent further, possibly permanent, physical damage when exposed to even a routine flight. As you will soon see, for humans, pressurized flight is truly an *unnatural act*.

## Putting On the Pressure

This may come as no surprise to most of you, but humans are basically full of hot air. Our bodies are essentially balloons, made of 70% water, with a vent on the top and another on the "bottom." On the ground we constantly experience very gradual pressure changes due to changing weather conditions. We also expose ourselves to changes in pressure when we travel over changes in elevation, as in a trip to the mountains. To experience the changes felt by the body on a typical one-hour flight, you'd have to drive your car up to an 8,000 foot mountain peak and back—and do so in about 45 minutes. Nowhere in nature does the human body experience the pressurization changes seen as rapidly as on a routine flight. Furthermore, we pressurize our insides by eating certain foods that produce gas.

The concept is simple: When you climb in altitude there is less pressure the higher you go. At sea level, the weight of the atmosphere above you exerts about 14 pounds of pressure on your body. Similar to the pressure you feel when you dive to the bottom of the swimming pool. The deeper you go, the more you feel. So, if you were to climb in an unpressurized plane to a high altitude (say for example, 10,000 feet) your body would be under less pressure than at sea level. Unfortunately, above 10,000 feet the air is pretty thin and the oxygen molecules in that air that our bodies need to function, are few and far between. Mountain climbers have to carry oxygen bottles to make it to the top of Mt. Everest, which is 29,000 ft high. A modern Jetliner flies as high as 43,000 feet. Not much oxygen is available up there.

> *Related Trivia Topic: The sparseness of air molecules at high altitude accounts for why jets go so fast at cruising altitude. Less air equals less drag. Just to keep the plane flying up high where the air molecules are fewer and farther apart, the wing has to move pretty quickly to hit enough of them to keep the plane aloft. That's good because the thinner air lets you get to your destination sooner.*

To keep passengers and crew alert (and alive) at altitude, you can either force-feed them oxygen under pressure as they sit in an unpressurized environment, not the most comfortable method, or, you can artificially pressurize their environment, allowing them to go about business as usual.

> *Yet More Trivia: No oxygen is released by the pressurization system. The system simply relies on pumping outside air into the plane under pressure. At altitude you are breathing the same air that is outside the plane. This is why when you fly through a cloud of smoke generated by a forest fire you can actually smell the wood smoke within the plane.*

The pressurization system in a modern jet aircraft initially maintains a cabin pressure slightly below the take-off airport elevation. As the plane climbs, the stress on the airframe posed by the pressurization system increases, like the air pressure on the wall of a balloon, until it reaches a maximum design limit. Then, the cabin starts to vent pressure (less cabin pressure equals higher altitude), to maintain no more than the maximum allowable pressure. We don't want the plane to pop like an over-inflated balloon and a pair of safety relief valves prevents this from happening. In a Boeing 737 flying at 37,000 feet, the cabin pressure reaches about 8,000 feet, like standing on a high mountain. The air pressure outside the aircraft is around 5 pounds per square inch. This difference between inside pressure and outside pressure, or "differential" as it is called, is a tremendous load borne by the aircraft fuselage—like a balloon straining to hold in air.

At 37,000 feet, the pressure holding the over-wing emergency exit hatches closed is over three tons. Ever wonder why there are no locks on airplane doors? You don't need them. *Ahh-nold* himself couldn't pry one of those things open when pressurized. The entry door is about four times the area of the exit hatch, and therefore sees upwards of *twelve tons* of pressure at cruising altitude. Next time you're boarding, check out the structure around the door area. We're talking *stout*. The 737 uses plug type doors in all locations, except the overwing exits on the newer models. Plug type doors close from the inside and actually seal tighter as the plane climbs. On doors that are not plug type, the opening mechanism is designed to work only if the cabin pressure is nearly equalized with that of outside the aircraft. For the record though, NEVER PLAY WITH A DOOR OR HATCH OPEN-ING MECHANISM ANYTIME EXCEPT WHEN DIRECTED TO BY A CREW-MEMBER OR AS INSTRUCTED TO DURING AN EMERGENCY. If you see anyone fiddling with an exit, tell them to stop and notify a crew-member immediately. Opening an exit without due cause will ensure you get to meet a host of law enforcement officials as well as a quick end to your trip.

> *Secret Pilot Stuff: Occasionally, a new pilot will set the wrong field elevation in the pressurization computer. As a result, upon landing the plane will overpressurize to a lower altitude which*

*means significantly more pressure inside the plane than outside the plane. In normal operation the pressurization does over-pressure slightly upon landing but this pressure equalizes in the time it takes the plane to taxi to the gate and the passengers never notice. In an extreme situation, the pressure may not have time to equalize. If you ever arrive at the gate and the Flight Attendants can't get the doors open and you notice your ears popping a little, this is why. The pressure inside is so great that the doors cannot be opened until the pressure inside the plane equalizes with that on the outside.*

The stresses the aircraft structure encounters from pressurization are far more damaging than those stresses it actually "feels" from flying. This is what ultimately does an airliner in after years of service. The repeated pressurization cycles cause cracks to form in the fuselage and at some point continued repairs become uneconomical. Ever notice the skin doubler patches around the entry doors as you enter the plane? Those are extra layers of metal over cracks that have formed from repeated pressurization stress. Don't worry, cracks in airplanes are absolutely normal. Refer back to Chapter 5 and read how maintenance finds and deals with these cracks. The whole point of this discussion of how pressurization affects the aircraft is to illustrate that you are under some stress as well as you sit in this pressurized environment. But unlike metal, at least your body stretches somewhat.

So, in normal flight on a pressurized airliner your body will travel as high as 8,000 feet. Once the cabin pressure begins to climb in altitude (go down in pressure), the rate is a very slow 200-300 feet per minute. Descents are a little faster but are usually not over 500 feet per minute—no big deal to most people. Vents in the inner ear and around the sinus cavities allow the pressure to equalize inside your body to match changing pressures outside the body.

Occasionally, when the airplane has descended very rapidly, the cabin pressure may get "behind." Normally, the pressurization system gets the cabin down to landing elevation by the time you land. Occasionally, the plane will descend faster than the pressurization system is programmed to repressurize. The result is loss of automatic cabin pressurization. This happens when a small pressure equalization door on the rear of the plane is forced open by the higher outside pressure, allowing the higher outside pressure to enter the cabin. As is often the case, the plane is usually still descending, and for the last few minutes before landing, the cabin rate of change in pressure will be the same as the aircraft's change in altitude. At this point the plane is basically unpressurized. If your ears are a little stuffed up you will notice this as you land because the change in pressure is slightly faster than normal.

On an unpressurized commuter plane, you will never climb higher than 10,000-12,000 feet because above this altitude the crew and passengers will need oxygen. The *rate* of climb and descent is controlled by how fast the plane climbs and descends. (Outside air pressure equals inside cabin pressure) Fortunately, all newer commuter aircraft are pressurized for your comfort.

# That Bloated Feeling

As you climb, Boyle's Law takes over your body, and as pressure on your anatomy is decreased, gasses within your body begin to expand in every cavity. As long as this pressure can escape, you experience little discomfort. Blocking these gasses and as the plane climbs to altitude, you may experience excruciating pain like you have never felt before. This pain will persist until you either return to a more pressurized environment (descend down in altitude) and Boyle's Law once again contains your internal pressures in equilibrium—or you vent the pressure.

An example:

One day, shortly after take-off, a gentleman passenger walked to the back of the plane and complained to the Flight Attendant that he was experiencing major pain in his lower abdominal area. She told him to sit on the Flight Attendant jumpseat for a second while she delivered her tray of drinks. When she returned, the passenger was on the floor doubled over in pain. He told the Flight Attendant that he needed to see a doctor immediately. Before she could call the pilots, the passenger got up saying, "I'm gonna die, we gotta land this plane. I have to tell the pilots." Before the Flight Attendant could stop him, he began to run towards the cockpit. As he started to run up the aisle, he began a loud "note" (for you non-musically trained readers, substitute the term "sphinctoral emission"). This "note" continued the *entire* length of the cabin to the front galley where he was met by a Flight Attendant who was prepared to block his attempt at cockpit access. Suddenly, relieved from his gastrointestinal pain, he gushed, "I can't believe it! I feel *fine* now!" Turning around, he faced all the aisle-seated passengers, freshly acquainted with the bouquet of what he had eaten the day before. The message is: Vent your gas before it becomes a problem. Anything that makes you produce gas on the ground will make you produce *even more* gas inflight. Try a gas relief medication an hour or more before the flight if you have experienced inflight bloating. I'm *told* this medication works pretty well.

On another flight, shortly after take-off, we got a call from the Flight Attendant in the rear of the cabin reporting that a female passenger reported smelling natural gas. As we continued to climb out, the smell in the rear became quite apparent and this lady passenger was gravely concerned that a natural gas leak somewhere was approaching an explosive level. The Flight Attendants in the rear of the cabin confirmed the strong smell.

Knowing that jetliners are not plumbed for natural gas, but fearing a possible leak from something in a passenger's luggage in the rear cargo area under the floor, we elected to return to the airport and have the problem checked out. As we descended the smell diminished. Canceling the flight and accommodating the passengers on the next flight, only a half an hour away, maintenance began to pore over the plane in search of the source of the odor.

As the passengers deplaned I noticed one sheepish gentleman who, coincidentally, had been seated right in front the lady who noticed the odor. As he walked by me, I too noticed the smell of "natural gas." We had been brought down by natural gas indeed—his. Too many fish tacos and beer the night before, I suspect. Or, some *bad buffet*. Either way, watch what you eat before you fly, as you will inevitably share the meal with those around you. The lady who noticed the smell wrote a glowing letter of thanks to my company outlining how the pilots had saved everyone's lives. I wanted to share my theory with her but my airline suggested otherwise.

Enough about gastro-intestinal misfortunes. These rarely pose much distress to the passenger: Well, maybe the passengers a few rows behind—remember the airflow in a jet is usually front to rear. Depressurizing the plane also affects the sinus cavities and the inner ear, both areas with very small vent tubes to the outside environment. More often, this is where most of the problems occur. Take a look at the following figures detailing these areas (see Figure 28).

The inner ear gets most attention. Think of the inner ear as a small balloon with the Eustachian tube being the neck of the balloon. As you climb, the higher pressure inside the inner ear normally vents out through the Eustachian tube into the throat. Yawning, swallowing and chewing gum will usually help in keeping the ears clear.

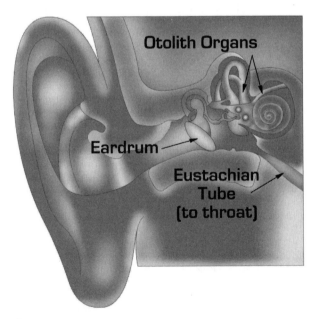

*Figure 28. The Inner Ear*

Often, the valsalva maneuver, holding your nose, closing your mouth, and blowing, can over-pressure the inner ear for a moment and help the ear begin to equalize. If nothing is done during climb the building pressure inside the middle ear usually overpowers the blockage and the ear clears by itself, like the balloon being partially inflated and then venting through the neck as the pressure is released. If the pressure building in the inner ear cannot escape, the pressure may, in extreme cases, rupture the eardrum. Any discomfort felt during climbout is an indication that more discomfort is headed your way once the plane has begun to descend.

The same is true for the sinuses (see Figure 29). Often, pressure will cause discomfort behind the eye or nose or forehead. These are unusual feelings you don't normally experience on the ground, unless you've experienced a really bad sinus headache. While these situations are uncomfortable, they are usually not as painful as those experienced when the ear or sinus is partially acclimated at a lower pressure during cruise flight and then blocks completely upon descent as air pressure tries to re-enter the sinuses. Descent is where most of the physical problems and damage occur.

## Descending Into Higher Pressure

As the plane begins the descent, the cabin pressure hesitates momentarily and then begins to slowly increase in pressure. All your body cavities that have equalized with the lower cabin pressure at cruise now slowly begin to repressurize to ground level. Air must now travel into your body through the tiny tubes and passages used to equalize pressure changes.

In the climb, the balloon structure of your ear vents higher-pressure air through the tiny Eustachian tube. Even with a mild blockage, the ear usually vents at least partially. An indication of partial blockage and inner ear over pressure is that plugged ear feeling and dim hearing. The pressure in your inner ear is pushing your ear drum out and preventing it from transmitting noise to your brain through it's normal vibration.

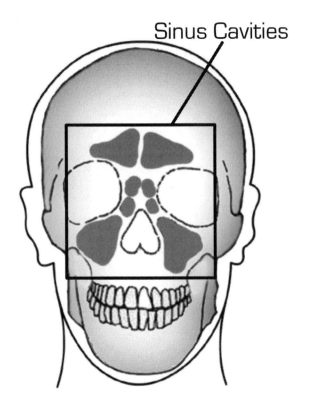

*Figure 29. The Sinus Cavities*

But, during descent, even a small blockage is worrisome because the air trying to get back into the inner ear through the Eustachian tube is forcing more of the sinus fluids and mucus from your throat into this tiny tube—like a cork. This often results in a dam of fluid or solid material that won't allow any air into the inner ear cavity. To make matters worse, some people have smaller than average Eustachian tubes. This is where most people experience discomfort.

If you feel any blockage at the start of descent, it's imperative that you try to keep your ears "up to speed" with the ever-changing cabin pressure. Yawning and wiggling your ear is fine if that works, but if neither one helps relieve your discomfort, definitely try the valsalva. You may have to blow pretty hard, but if you keep equalizing the pressure in little steps as you feel your ear discomfort, you'll stand a better chance of getting down to earth without tearing your eardrum. You may not get your ears completely cleared by landing, but at least your discomfort will be minimized.

From the *Air Force Aerospace Physiology* textbook:

"Equalizing pressure during descent can be accomplished by swallowing, yawning, tensing the muscles in the throat, moving the head from side to side (*to stretch the Eustachian tubes a bit*) extending the jaw or performing the valsalva maneuver. Using the valsalva maneuver, air can be forced into the middle ear by closing the mouth, pinching the nose closed and forcibly exhaling. This method opens the Eustachian tube and equalizes the pressure differential between the middle ear and the atmosphere. Some pilots find that they must valsalva frequently during descent without waiting for a sensation of discomfort. Others find that the valsalva maneuver can be used as soon as they recognize discomfort such as fullness or ringing of the ears, decreased ability to hear, or pain."

Perforating an eardrum is what happens when the outside air pressure finally overpowers the tiny eardrum membrane and rips a hole or tear in it. The sensation feels for a split second like someone just stuck an ice pick through your eardrum. Fortunately, the damage heals quickly, in 3-5 weeks, with only minor effects on your hearing. But, if at all possible, you want to avoid getting into this situation in the first place. An ear block *hurts!*

The same is true for a sinus blockage. These pains are very sharp and feel like an ice pick is poking you from inside your skull. Valsalvas can often relieve them entirely, depending on which sinus is involved—and why it's bothered in the first place. Sinus infections as well as inner ear infections often involve swollen tissue already upset before pressurization/depressurization serving to block paths of escape and entry for air pressure.

Once, I had a sinus blockage right behind my nose. At the time I jokingly called it a "nose block," but as the cabin got closer to landing elevation the pain really began to mount. I was flying the aircraft at the time and figured "We'll be on the ground in just a minute and I'll take care of the problem there." Whoa buddy! Did that thing start to hurt! At the moment I landed the aircraft on the runway I heard a long groan in my sinus cavity as it equalized, and the pain vanished. Before this flight I had felt no indications of any sinus upset whatsoever.

## Ray Finally Gets To The Point

The moral of the story is: If you suspect you may have some kind of major cold or other malady going on inside your head and you are about to fly on a plane—CHECK WITH YOUR DOCTOR BEFORE FLYING. If that is impossible, then try to alleviate the symptoms with over the counter medications, but make sure you have some nasal sinus spray, Afrin or similar, in case you develop a blockage. I never fly without a bottle of Afrin handy, and it has come in handy for fellow crewmembers many times. Afrin helps melt mucous that blocks the passages. If you have a history of problems with ear blocks from previous flights—SEE A DOCTOR. *Especially* if you feel like you are experiencing a cold.

Now that you know all about why your ears pop, here are a few more suggestions to make traveling on a plane a little safer and a whole lot more enjoyable.

1. Drink lots of water before you fly. Don't get silly here, but do hydrate yourself before flying. The humidity level at cruise on an airplane is lower than nearly any place on earth and just breathing will suck the moisture right out of your body; just remember to use the restroom *before* you board the plane. Drink some water on the plane too.

2. Avoid alcohol. I know some people can't imagine flying without a full tray of Bloody Mary's in their lap, but try to be reasonable. People who get ripped just to fly are going to be unable to help themselves in an emergency. Furthermore, in

the highly unlikely event your plane depressurizes at altitude, you will probably pass out in mere seconds. The time of useful consciousness at 35,000 feet is about 30 seconds for someone without alcohol in his or her system. One beer drastically reduces that valuable time to don your oxygen mask or make it back to your seat if moving about the cabin. Same for you "Valium Flyers." Everybody knows you "rent" beer, you don't buy it, and that dehydrates you further. Drink water. Save the booze for when you get there. And, especially avoid alcohol if you are seated next to the emergency exits. The folks around you are counting on your good judgment and coordination to get the emergency exit open should the need arise. Your fellow passengers will not appreciate you opening an emergency exit when there's fire outside. FAA regulation denies access onboard an aircraft to anyone *suspected* of being under the influence of alcohol. Look ripped and smell like a brewery and you probably won't be allowed to board. Get hammered inflight and you'll likely be asked to deplane. Why the FAA, in its infinite wisdom, allows passengers seated in the overwing exit rows to drink alcohol, is beyond me.

3.  Don't eat a huge meal right before you get on a plane or after you get airborne. Airlines aren't known for banquets anyway. Processing a large meal draws blood away from your other organs and this contributes to hydration problems as well as reduced ability to function in an oxygen deficient atmosphere. Again, be reasonable. Equate eating a big meal and then getting on a plane to that feeling you have after donating blood.

4.  If you are flying with infants, don't put a bottle of milk in their mouth during descent and then lay them down. The bottle helps them clear their ears by swallowing for sure, but the milk stands a chance of getting pumped into their Eustachian tubes during descent, and that virtually guarantees an ear infection a few days later. *You* don't need that, especially if you plan to fly home another day with your child. Sit them upright with a bottle of water or a pacifier during descent.

5. Always keep a set of foam earplugs handy. The plugs really helps cut the noise, especially in the back of the plane, and helps you nap or concentrate on that book. But, should the need arise, you can still hear commands or announcements given by the crew.

6. If you are prone to motion sickness, sit by a window forward of the wing, preferably up near the front. Hopefully, looking out the window will provide you with a reference that will correct for some of the exaggerated otolith stimulation (inner ear balance, see next section) which contributes to motion sickness. Sitting in an aisle seat in mild turbulence, you would swear the plane is rolling upside down. A glance outside tells you it's not nearly as bad as it feels.

A study years back identified two types of people: Those termed "lazy eyed" and those termed "sharp eyed." This naming had nothing to do with the clarity of their vision. The study revealed that in some people who suffered from motion sickness, their brains worked extremely hard at trying to keep their eyes following the changing movement about them, which in turn induced motion sickness in these individuals. These people were termed the "sharp eyes." Their brains produced the nausea feeling if they were unable to visually lock onto an object that was not moving. In other words, still objects could be tracked by the moving eye, and thus reduce or eliminate the motion sickness. Looking out the window is a great way to watch things that are relatively still.

For the "lazy eyes," their brain could handle a momentary difference in what the otolith organs were telling the brain versus what the eyes were telling the brain, regarding their position. These subjects were shown to have eyes that didn't try to follow the movements as aggressively, and, somehow that eliminated or minimized their tendency to suffer motion sickness. Try sitting by a window and looking outside if you are prone to feeling nauseous inflight. I am a "sharp eye" and if I try to read a newspaper in the van on the way to the hotel, I get nauseous. Either I look out the window inflight, or I take a nap. Strangely, bumps lull me to sleep if I have had a hard day with little sleep the night before.

7. Another good reason to sit up front and by a window is that the autopilot package is located beneath the floor, by the front galley. This package is the motion-sensing portion of the auto-pilot. This device responds to turbulence by moving control surfaces on the plane in an attempt to correct for turbulence. The back of the plane—where the flight controls are—is moving all over the place trying to give the autopilot package a smooth ride. Sit up front and enjoy the better ride. (Amazingly, the autopilot three-axis gyro package is modeled after the otolith organs inside our inner ears. See the next section.)

8. If you do any type of compressed-air diving underwater, give yourself at least 24 hours before climbing on a jet for home. Otherwise, a harmless cabin pressurization problem may result in a serious case of the bends.

9. If you find that you need oxygen during the flight, a passenger oxygen cylinder will be made available to you. But, be aware that most airlines will have you removed at the next stop as your health and well-being are now in question. Liability concerns require that you visit a doctor to seek a medical release before continuing your trip.

Keep your arms inside the ride at all times!

While we are talking about flying and its effect on the body, I want to mention the otolith organs. They are the semi-circular canals in your inner ear that tell you where up and down is as well as give you a sensation of movement. Flying makes these things "lie like mad" and if you know what to look for, you can catch them in the act.

Otolith organs are comprised of three small circular canals located inside each ear. Each canal is set on one of the three axes—pitch, roll, and yaw. Each canal is filled with a fluid that momentarily remains stationary as your head moves. Inside each circular canal are tiny hairs that bend under the flow of the moving fluid producing the sensation of movement (see Figure 30).

Forward acceleration on the human body makes the organs think they are starting to go uphill because the little hairs inside the canals bend under acceleration forces as they normally would under pressure from the flowing fluid in the canals. Next time you take-off, stare at the bulkhead at the front in the cabin and see if you don't feel like the plane is starting up a hill as the acceleration starts. Conversely, when decelerating upon landing, you will feel like you are going downhill. A peek out the window will confuse your brain even more! As you rotate your head 45 degrees to look out the window you'll feel like you are leaning! Acceleration affects the hairs in a different direction as you turn your head. Even things outside may momentarily look like they are leaning in the direction the plane is

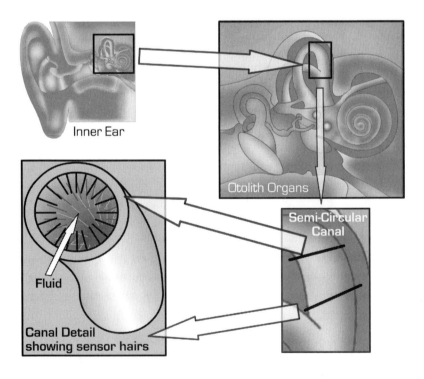

*Figure 30. Otolith Organs*

going as your poor brain tries to figure out what the heck is going on. That confused feeling of your inner ear telling you something your brain doesn't quite believe is called cognitive dissonance. Cool eh? Pilots are trained to ignore these conflicting sensations. This confusion is exactly why pilots must obey their instruments. The human balance system is not designed to handle routine accelerations experienced inflight. Remember those birds I told you about who hold above or between clouds layers rather than fly in them? They must suffer from the same problems we do and they know they must wait until they can see the ground before trying to land. We owe a great debt to those early aviation pioneers who designed, developed and tested instruments that allow us to safely fly in clouds.

That completes our peek into Aerospace Physiology. I'm not trying to make a doctor out of you. I'm just trying to provide a little of the "owners manual" info passengers really need, but rarely get. Millions of people fly every year with little or no problems. Physiologically speaking though, flying is truly an unnatural' event. More informed people like you may now recognize the symptoms of inflight physiological problems as they begin to occur—-and how to relieve them before they pose a problem.

*After flying home to spend Christmas with his parents, a passenger met his suitcase stuffed with gifts at the carousel. As it bumped down the baggage ramp, it half opened and his toothbrush fell out. Hastily retrieving his suitcase, he couldn't catch up with the toothbrush. As it continued around the baggage carrousel he overheard a passenger say, "My, that person travels light."*

# 10:

# Aviation Security

**All** one can say about aviation security at this point is that this "necessary evil" is a constantly developing story. For me to share my opinion or make suggestions would be like shooting at a moving target. Much has been done by the federal agencies involved but there is still much more to accomplish. Whatever aspect I would comment on now would hopefully be improved by the time you read this. As this book is meant to serve as a reference tool for the flier, I won't chock these pages full of useless and soon-to-be-out-of-date information that would inevitably bore you.

What I will say is the commentary by the experts and the media in the editorial sections of the nation's newspapers and on news talk shows is very accurate. The government is very good at creating bureaucracy and the one begun after September 11, 2001 is the largest single governmental entity created in our lifetime. When have you ever heard the terms "government" and "efficient" used in the same sentence? We now live with an 800-pound gorilla that fashions every aspect of aviation security. Let's hope he stays awake, and on the job—and doesn't need glasses.

You have probably heard enough about security issues to form a pretty good opinion of what has been done thus far, and what is needed to ensure a better job of screening passengers and baggage. The fact that you bought this book seeking more information means you probably are aware of the current state of affairs regarding aviation security issues. You are especially aware if you flew a few times in the year after the September 11th attacks and witnessed first-hand the variance in procedures and levels of attention offered by the different airports across this nation.

Let me set the record straight: The airlines are out of the security business now and every rule, procedure, and requirement is clearly spelled out by the federal government, namely the Transportation Security Agency (TSA). The airlines must follow the TSA guidelines. So, if you experience or witness any questionable security practices, don't be quick to blame your airline. Until the TSA takes over all the airports in this country, there will be small differences in procedures, but shortly, all security procedures will be uniformly administered throughout the country. If you have a complaint, ask the supervisor at the security checkpoint how you can file a complaint regarding your treatment or handling. Filing a formal complaint does have an effect. You may include a copy to your airline and this helps the airline develop a casebook if certain members of the security agency are doing a less than stellar job, but remember: The airlines are customers of the TSA just like we passengers and crews.

I won't placate you. Security requirements are a hassle, plain and simple, whether for the passenger or the crew. Don't think that, just because crewmembers are in uniform, we don't get our share of "attention" from security. Occasionally being singled out for further inspection is inconvenient but necessary. I still cling to my belief that we need *smarter* security, not *more* security. For those of you who fly frequently and have a suggestion or a complaint, I encourage you to voice your concerns to those who can make a difference. Congress controls the TSA, as well as the FAA and DOT, and is keenly interested in your concerns. Remember, congressmen fly back to their home states, sometimes weekly, and they endure the same occasionally inane handling by security personnel as the rest of us. Simply writing your elected leaders in Washington, D.C. will have an incredible effect. Stay interested, stay informed, and stay *involved*.

The *key* to making sure we have the most efficient and effective security system is your involvement. Get your friends and relatives to contact their congressmen as well. Don't accept eyewash: Write and call your legislators in Washington. Your efforts *will* make a difference in making the aviation security system better and more efficient.

How can you help? The best way to convey your concerns is by visiting your congressional representative in person. Secondly, write your congressmen in Washington. Send them letters and then follow up with phone calls to both their local offices and their offices in Washington D.C. Writing the TSA, DOT, and FAA heads will help them understand the groundswell of support the public places behind making the changes to make the system of aviation security in this country more efficient and effective.

## How to Get in Touch

**Senate:** Simply go to www.senate.gov and follow the links to identify the Senators from your state along with their Washington D.C. office addresses.

**House of Representatives:** Go to www.house.gov/house/MemberWWW.html and enter your state and zip code information to find your Representative. Then, by simply clicking on their name, you will be linked to that representative's web site, which will have office addresses as well as e-mail information.

For those without access to a computer, simply refer to the Government section of your White Pages in your telephone directory. There, under "Congress," you will find the addresses and phone numbers for local offices of Senators and Representatives that represent you. Or call the Congressional operator at (202) 224-3121 and ask for the Washington D.C. office for Senators and Representatives from your state.

The chief at the TSA is James M. Loy. His address is:

James M. Loy
Transportation Security Administration
400 Seventh Street SW
Washington D.C. 20590
TSA phone: 866-289-9673

The current head of the Department of Transportation is Norman Y. Mineta and his address is:

Secretary Norman Mineta
U.S. Department of Transportation
400 7th Street, SW
Washington D.C. 20590
Information at (202) 366-4000.

The current chief of the Federal Aviation Administration is Marion Clifton Blakey. You can share your concerns with her at:

Marion C. Blakey
Federal Aviation Administration
800 Independence Avenue, S.W.
Washington, DC 20591

In your letter, describe what you experienced as you traveled, how that experience could have been better or simply point out what you think is wrong with the current security system. In each letter you write, be sure to tell each agency you want to see *smarter* security, not necessarily *more* security. If the hurdle presented by airline security gets any higher, there won't be any airlines left in business because the passengers will have driven their cars. We can't stand the usual glacial governmental response time either.

Channel your frustration into action! I find writing cathartic, especially if doing so may actually do some good. Believe it or not, a thousand letters on a given topic to a congressman rings alarm bells. Ten thousand letters leave the congressional staffers drop-jawed. Remember, the staffers schedule the congressmen and women every day! With millions of air travelers flying throughout this country every year, if only one in a hundred passengers wrote their legislators, we'd all see faster and more efficient movement on the part of the government. We in the industry can't change the current system by ourselves. We need your help.

# Should We Fly? Is It Safe?

This whole discussion of security is simply an extension of the discussion of risk assessment we began earlier in this book: In every undertaking in life there is a risk and we must take measures to minimize those risks. Does the current security environment mean you shouldn't fly? No, absolutely not. Measured across the millions of people who fly every day, the additional risk associated with terrorism is miniscule. But, like every aspect of aviation that has been improved throughout history, we must bolster aviation security to minimize the threat. To give in to fear not only paralyzes us as individuals or countrymen, but also sends the signal to the terrorists that they have won. I, and millions of other Americans, have made the decision to continue going about our everyday lives as usual. We are more aware and cautious but we are not in any way giving in to those who seek to destroy our very way of life.

## From "The American Crisis"

*"These are times that try men's souls. The summer soldier and the sunshine patriot will, in this crisis, shrink from the service of their country, but he that stands it now, deserves the love and thanks of man and woman. Tyranny, like hell, is not easily conquered; yet we have this consolation with us, that the harder the conflict, the more glorious the triumph. What we obtain too cheap, we esteem to lightly: It is dearness only that gives everything its value. Heaven knows how to put a proper price upon its goods; and it would be strange indeed if so celestial an article as freedom should not be highly rated."*

*—Thomas Paine, 1776*

*The beginning of knowledge is the discovery*
*of something we do not understand.*

—Frank Herbert (1920-1986)

# Perspective

## "Folks, this is your Captain again. We have begun our descent...."

**As** I close this effort to help you, the commercial flier, I am again greeted by new reports of an aircraft accident. This one involves a single business jet where 18 passengers and crew perished in Colorado.

Not surprisingly, CNN is carrying the preliminary news conference live with occasional cuts to scenes of burning wreckage. The fire isn't yet out and the news reporters at this conference want the National Transportation and Safety Board representative to explain what happened. Moreover, the investigation has not yet begun and the tone of the reporter's questioning suggests that they want immediate answers as to what caused the accident.

Again, I am compelled to ask myself, "If these poor souls were lost in a bus accident, would that even make the news?" Perhaps a train wreck is newsworthy because they seem to happen so infrequently. Is it the infrequent occurrence of plane crashes that catapult them onto the front page? Or, a lingering distrust of a complex and misunderstood transportation system; one that had a steep learning curve at its onset but since has proven itself over time to be the safest mode of transportation yet created?

Or, is it a generational thing? I remember older relatives saying they would never fly in a plane. Now, flying has become mundane, even to the point of being despised because of its disappointments; a system with finite capacity clogged with more and more flyers. Could a lingering doubt remain to those in my generation and to the latest generation hence, because of comments made by our parents and elders? I believe so. But I believe fear of flying is a far more complex issue than simply fanning the flames of some fear harbored by an older relative or friend. The fears we experience spring from a host of issues, not the least of which is fear in general: Fear of not being in control. Or fear of being involved in some major calamity that takes our lives. If these are fearful times, then it is only natural that some of that fear is projected wherever we go. But are we being truly honest with ourselves?

As passengers, we sweat out a bumpy flight only to relax later as we drive home oblivious to the fact that simply by getting out of a plane and into a car, we have increased our chances of being killed by a factor of more than 20. The comfort of the friendly and familiar surroundings of the family car has lulled us into complacency. We think to ourselves, "Now I am in control again." Do we stop to think about all the other drivers we share the highway with? People frequently drive home from the airport after a drink or two on the plane, seemingly unaware that alcohol affects their ability to operate their automobile. Cell phone use while driving is reportedly as much a contributor to vehicle accidents as attempting to drive under the influence—yet we do it, often without thinking. Could it be the unfamiliar experience of getting on a plane that sends many people into cold sweats?

Think about this for a minute: We do insane things to ourselves to reduce our chances of contracting this ailment or that illness by a factor of less than 100%. You probably take vitamin supplements with the hope that they will reduce the chances of Alzheimer's, Parkinson's or some other malady by some percentage. I do too. Yet do we really comprehend the fact that by driving to San Francisco as opposed to flying there, we have increased our chances of dying by over 2,000 percent?

Hopefully this mindset will change with education, largely aided by the media. Why then doesn't the media champion the incredible safety record of commercial aviation? The media's aversion to reality seems to me rather disingenuous when they point out one negative fact regarding our personal safety while disregarding another positive one. A media representative might counter, "That's what people want to see when they turn on the news. They want the facts right now and it is our job to give it to them." I'll agree we need reporting, I just wish the information presented could be more balanced and fair. Given the safety record of commercial flight, reminding the public about how incredibly safe flying has become might help assuage fears brought on by video of burning wreckage. But, I'm a pilot. What do I know?

One television show that got my blood pressure up was thinly veiled expose on why planes crash. Under the guise of a news or educational documentary was a one sided discussion into several noteworthy accidents. Even the actress who hosted the show admitted that she was afraid of flying. Everything she covered in the show was designed to alarm and incite fear or raise questions. Nowhere did she offer explanation to what circumstances might have contributed to the accident, nor did she offer any lessons learned afterwards. In one incident they chronicled, I know for a fact they totally misstated the real cause. They were flat out wrong. This show and the many others like it have done much to sensationalize a tiny portion of the story of commercial aviation. During coverage of the next aircraft accident, be very aware of what you are being told by the media and how they are presenting the story. Are they being balanced in bringing you established facts along with creditable eyewitness reports? Or when they tell you that the airplane involved had undergone an engine replacement the week prior are they telling you this is a routine event, something that happens with regularity in commercial aviation? Does the media coverage inform you and educate you as to what is normal and what is irregular? Or, does their report leave more questions in your mind?

The print media does a far better job of distilling the facts before going to press to report a crash. They have the luxury of time to think about what data to present as opposed to the live nature of television, which often presents a strikingly powerful and indelible image with little context within which to measure its value. Microphones that appear moments after an aircraft crash are often nowhere to be seen a year or so later when the accident investigation team has finished a thorough and detailed examination of what actually happened. Perhaps I shouldn't crucify the television media. They are getting better. As a professional within this industry, I remain supremely annoyed to see leading questions asked, often in a disdainful manner, of a member of the aviation community to the point of insinuating that the person being questioned is "hiding something" from the reporter. Or similarly worse, dragging some purported "aviation expert" on camera to further some off-tangent theory which ultimately bears little relation to the facts, once they are revealed by investigation. There are so many creditable people in aviation and for some reason many TV networks can't seem to find one when the need arises. Perhaps they should have people on staff who have a background in commercial aviation and can put facts or details into meaningful perspective for the viewers at home. Some of the most insightful and accurate comments I have seen regarding aviation accidents have come from the news chopper pilots covering the scene. Discussing something as complex as an accident will take more than the allotted two-minute time slot between commercials however.

Do not mistake what I am saying. Aircraft accidents are terrible events and they are newsworthy. But we shouldn't want to scare the devil out of the flying public with gory images and little useful information. Recent television coverage since 9-11 has been much more factual and educational. I hope this trend continues.

I guess risk aversion comes down to one's beliefs about life in general. Everyone has his or her own threat threshold and comfort level. I want you, the reader, to come away from this examination of flying with the understanding that commercial aviation has made enormous strides in improving safety over the past fifty years. As professionals, we have endeavored to learn from our mistakes, and institute measures and procedures to prevent reoccurrence of accidents. There will always be a small measure of risk involved with flying. This risk simply has to be measured against activities we undertake daily without any thought or concern. Try to keep every-thing you hear and learn in perspective. Only then will we understand how truly safe commercial aviation is. As I previously mentioned, I started out my affiliation with aviation as a child flying with my father. Though I had some initial concerns or questions about the safety of this endeavor, the more I learned the more my fears were put to rest. In over twenty years as a professional aviator I have found no reason to change my opinion about flying one bit.

As you prepare to travel by air for business or pleasure, I want you to look back on all the topics we have covered together and take great reassurance in knowing that the plane you fly in is over-designed for the task of flying you and your loved ones to your destination. The aircraft is maintained by dedicated people who themselves fly on the same planes. If you encounter some weather along your route of flight, as long as you have your seatbelt fastened, you'll come through any bumps along the way in fine shape. Your pilots and crew have trained for all manner of occurrences and are prepared to take measures to ensure you arrive safely at your destina-tion. By listening to their instructions and suggestions, you maximize your chances of survival should something unusual happen.

Those still frozen in fear at the thought of flying will need further help. The programs and resources listed in the Appendix are but a start. The important thing is to make the crucial first step in trying to get help. Until then, you will continue to be out of control of your life and unable to enjoy the freedoms that trust and understanding offer.

For the rest of us, rather than to dwell on the "maybes" and "might happens," I wish you would relax for a moment and realize the freedom that air travel offers in the ability to cover vast distances in a very short amount of time. A jetliner truly is a "time machine." Over a lifetime of flight, I still pause in wonderment every time I lift off this green Earth. I understand most of the technical explanations and science that goes into flight but it still seems like a miracle when I see it happen. (How can the same breath I blow on my hand hold up a 500 ton jetliner?) Don't pine over worries about the aircraft. If you hear a noise or see something odd, re-read Chapter 3. Don't worry about flight delays or arrival times. Worrying won't get you there any sooner. Forget about your luggage arriving at your destination. Chances are excellent that your bags will be waiting for you. In the end, your worrying doesn't help a thing. Sit back and enjoy flying for the miracle that it is. And, understand how incredibly safe flying is, compared to the other daily activities we undertake routinely.

May the winds be at your back, may the ride be smooth, and may your touchdowns be soft.

I hope to see you on my aircraft someday.

Captain Ray Stark

# Appendix:

# Additional Help With Anxiety

*"To continue to live with your fear is to confine yourself in a self-made prison."*

—Lloyd Douglas

The American Psychological Association reports that one out of every 75 people experience some level of Panic Disorder. Evidence indicates there may be a genetic predisposition toward panic disorders, which are generally triggered by some stressful event or period in the person's life. For unknown reasons women are twice as likely to experience this disorder. Symptoms may range from an increased level of general concern all the way to full blown panic attacks.

A panic attack is a "sudden surge of overwhelming fear that comes without warning and without any obvious reason." It is believed that stress lowers your resistance to anxiety and the underlying predisposition kicks in and triggers the attack. The mere act of traveling—packing bags, leaving loved ones, going to unfamiliar places, these all certainly place the traveler under some measure of stress, which may trigger an attack. The key to resolving this disorder is receiving the level of treatment commensurate with your level of anxiety.

Whether your concern is simply the act of flying or whether flying triggers anxiety over other concerns, there are a host of programs and resources to help you. Some may be as simple as a self-help book available at the local bookstore or online. Other programs are more detailed, involving not only reading but also audio or video-taped materials, which augment the written information. These programs are handy because audio tapes can be played in your car while commuting to and from work and in combination with the written information you can read in your off time, allow you to cover quite a bit of information in a short period of time. Plus, audiotapes listened to regularly over a long period help reinforce learning that brings about real change.

The next step beyond self-help is actually visiting a facility designed to help you overcome your fears. Some are dedicated to specific fears (fear of flying courses) while others involve one-on-one counseling over an extended period of time. Your choice as to which route to take is not as important as actually taking the first all-important step to try and get help. When you do, you'll realize that you are not sick, mentally ill or in any way different from the estimated 30 million others who share anxiety and depression symptoms. Most of all, you will quickly realize, YOU ARE NOT ALONE.

## Local Fear of Flying Classes:

Local fear of flying classes are usually held on a quarterly basis in larger cities. Usually, these classes are taught by airline employees on their off time, or other individuals, with either flying or psychiatric credentials—or both. Tracking them down is often tricky. Most major airlines do not offer fear of flying classes but may be able to refer you to one held in your area. Call your local airline office or your local airport information number about availability in your area. Your doctor may have information on where classes are held in your locale.

## National programs:

S.O.A.R.
Seminars On Aeroanxiety Relief      1-800-332-7539
P.O. Box 747
Westport, CT 06881
www.fearofflying.com

SOAR offers a three step course dealing with psychology of fear, aviation information and practice. Counseling by telephone with founder Capt. Tom Bunn, a licensed therapist, is one helpful aspect of this program. Program offers a money back guarantee.

Flight Anxiety Treatment Program—Fear Takes Flight
http://feartakesflight.com
L. Jay Koch, M.S.W., L.S.C.S.W.     816-651-5700
Plaza Time Building
Medical Office Suite 251
411 Nichols Road
Kansas City, MO 64112

A multi-step in-house program located in Kansas City, Missouri. where you set your own goals and develop stress resolution techniques culminating in an aircraft flight with your therapist-pilot. Covers anxiety management and reduction as well as aviation related information and other relevant data. Therapy done weekly with aircraft desensitization done over weekends. Telephone consultations may be available on a case-by-case basis. Plan is tailored to meet your specific needs.

Lucinda Bassett
The Midwest Center for Stress and Anxiety
1-800-944-9428
Midwest Center
P.O. Box 205
Oak Harbor, OH 43449
www.stresscenter.com

The Midwest Center offers a complete and comprehensive array of tools to help those with anxieties of all types. Founder Lucinda Bassett, once a fearful flyer, has since developed a program to help the individuals calm anxieties and conquer fears, once again taking control of their lives. Course materials include written material, audio and videotapes. Programs covered by 30-day money-back guarantee. Website offers contact with people who are taking or have taken the course. Developed through 17 years of clinical therapy groups. Used by over 500,000 people worldwide. Featured on *Oprah, Maury Povich, Montel Williams, The View, Barbara Walters.*

Web information:

National Institute of Mental Health (NIMH)
http://www.nimh.nih.gov/anxiety/

Mental Health Net
http://anxiety.mentalhelp.net/

American Psychological Association
http://www.apa.org/pubinfo/panic.html

# Aviation Glossary

**aileron**          The moveable portion of the trailing edge on the outermost section of the wing which allows the plane to bank. When up, it acts like a spoiler, which "spoils" or lessens lift generated by the wing. When tilted down, it acts like a flap increasing the lift produced by the wing by increasing the "camber" or underside curvature of the wing. Ailerons on most aircraft act in opposite directions while banking the aircraft, adding lift on one wing while removing some lift from the opposite wing, allowing the plane to bank and turn.

**airframe**          The structure making up the aircraft, the fuselage, wings, and tail.

**airspeed**          The speed at which air is moving across the surfaces of the aircraft. May not equal speed at which aircraft crosses the ground (groundspeed) due to winds aloft.

**airworthiness release**          Signature by maintenance personnel in aircraft logbook signifying that aircraft logbook meets requirements for flight. Must be accomplished every seven days. Certain aircraft discrepancies require a new airworthiness release to be accomplished before flight.

**alley**                Often used by pilots to describe the taxiway between concourses and their respective jetways. "Folks, we're holding short of the alley for outbound traffic...." meaning another aircraft has pushed back from its gate and there is insufficient room for your aircraft to taxi by this aircraft en route to your gate.

**alternate**       Another airport chosen as a substitute destination should landing at your original intended destination become impossible or unwise due to weather, ATC problems, or mechanical difficulty. In cases of low visibility weather or passing thunderstorms/snowstorms/etc, an alternate is always planned for and must have better weather than the original destination. Extra fuel is carried to fly to the original destination and then to the alternate. Take-off alternates are used in low visibility situations where the visibility is good enough to take off but not high enough to allow for a return to the departure airport.

**approach**      The procedure the pilot uses to guide the plane through weather using instruments remaining clear of terrain obstacles to a point near the end of the runway where, if visibility allows, the pilot will land the aircraft upon seeing the runway. If the runway is not sighted, the pilot will continue to fly the go-around portion of the approach to remain clear of terrain for either a subsequent approach attempt or a divert to another airport. Also short for approach control, the ATC agency tasked with the landing phase of traffic control.

**APU**               Auxiliary Power Unit. The small jet engine, usually in the rear of the fuselage, which provides electrical power and pneumatic bleed (air pressure) to run the heater/air conditioner.

**ATC**                    Air Traffic Control. The arm of the Federal Aviation Administration that talks to the pilots and clears them to taxi, take-off, fly en route, and land. ATC is defined by zones of control (tower, approach, departure, center or high altitude). ATC's primary job is to ensure aircraft remain clear of one another and clear of the ground (mountains, hills, TV towers, etc.). Control of aircraft within 5 miles of the airport is maintained by the control tower at the airport. Departure and Approach control handles the traffic between airport towers and Center controllers. En route control (once the plane is above approximately 13,000 feet) is maintained by different "center" controllers en route; i.e., Albuquerque Center, L.A. Center, Ft. Worth Center, etc. which control vast regions of the country. Not all airports or airspace is controlled by ATC. ATC control is limited to the major airports in most major cities and altitudes above 18,000 feet.

**ATC flow**       A program where-by aircraft departures are metered (delayed like the red/green meter light on freeway on-ramps.) This programs controls aircraft departing countrywide for airports where congestion is experienced or anticipated. ATC Flow eliminates all the planes from arriving at the same destination at once and provides for less chance of holding as the plane nears its destination.

**autopilot**      A device which smoothly flies the aircraft under supervision of the pilot, relieving the pilot workload and allowing the pilot to focus attention on matters of importance (weather, holding, etc). Despite common misperceptions, the pilot actually flies the aircraft but does so usually by means of inputs to the autopilot.

| | |
|---|---|
| **bleed air** | High pressure, high temperature air "bled" off the turbine compressor section for use in running air conditioning/heater packs for heating/cooling of the aircraft. Also used for anti-ice systems on wing leading edge and engine anti-ice. |
| **borescope** | A viewing device which allows maintenance personnel to look down a long, thin, flexible tube allowing a look inside an assembled engine or other piece of equipment being inspected. |
| **camber** | The "curvature" of the underside of the wing surface (see Figure 12). Flaps change camber to increase the lift produced by the wings for take-off and landing. This effect is the felt when you hold your flat hand (fingertips forward) out the window of a moving car and then begin to slightly "cup" your hand, increasing the lift. |
| **carrier** | An airline industry term used for an airline company. Delta, American, and United are all "carriers." |
| **center** | Short for ATC agency controlling mid and high altitude airspace. |
| **center of gravity** | Where the plane would balance from if suspended at that point. |
| **center of lift** | A point where the sum total of lift from a wing is focused. |
| **company** | An industry term for a jet of the same company. A pilot might say to the tower controller "Roger, United 123 will follow company to runway 12," meaning one United plane will follow another United plane to runway 12. |
| **contract maintenance** | Maintenance acquired at a location where the airline has no maintenance of its own. Usually only does minor repairs to get the aircraft back to carriers home maintenance facility. |

**controllers**     Refers to Air Traffic Controllers who oversee and manage the movement of aircraft across the country.

**dadgum**     Adjective describing ill-timed occurrence or other less than desirable traits as in "The dadgum hooty-honker is all whompyjawed." syn: dad-blamed, doggone, darned.

**dispatch**     Airline dispatch personnel who sit in a consolidated office and monitor the airfield equipment status, and actual aircraft en route via radar downlink from the FAA as well as real-time weather radar, airport weather reports, and satellite photos from the National Weather Service. Dispatchers also provide communications help with maintenance and deal with a myriad of issues including aircraft weight and balance concerns and aircraft holding and divert decisions. Simply put, Dispatchers are the pilot's biggest aid on the ground. (I call them "Mother" because they worry about a zillion details that could affect their jets en route.)

**divert**     The act of flying the aircraft to an alternate destination. May be the result of weather, runway closure at the destination, equipment failure at the destination or other reason.

**engine pylon**     The support structure attached to the wing or fuselage which attaches the engine to the plane.

**FAA**     The Federal Aviation Administration, a government agency dedicated to managing the air traffic control system and all pieces of that system from pilot licensing to aircraft inspection and rule enforcement. Their primary charge is to ensure the system operates with the most practical level of safety possible.

**FARs**               Federal Aviation Regulations. Rules that deal with every aspect of aviation in the U.S.

**first gust**       That wind generated by cold air falling out of the bottom of a mature thunderstorm. Usually generates the dust storm common to large thunderstorms.

**flight release**   A form issued by the airline which contains important information about the status of navaids, airport facilities, winds and weather expected to be encountered en route, as well as the specific routing the flight will follow, what altitude it will fly, as well as any possible alternate airport information if necessary.

**flaps**             The panels on the inner portion of the rear of the wing. These panels produce more camber (curve) to the wing and thereby produce more lift. Special panels on the inboard (closest to the cabin) section of the front of the wing on many planes are also called "leading edge flaps." The outer most portions of the leading (forward) edge are called "slats". See Figures 12, 23.

**flight plan**     The form showing the detailed, leg-by-leg routing the plane will follow from take-off to landing.

**flow time**      A time specifying a two-minute take-off window for the orderly flow of aircraft to your destination. Issued by ATC Flow Control in Washington D.C. Think of it a predetermined space you'll need to blend into morning rush hour freeway traffic. If you miss this time it usually means delays. Also called "slot times" or simply "flow."

**go around**      The flight procedure whereby the pilot flies away from the ground when the runway is not sighted on approach or when the runway is not clear ahead or for some reason the approach has not placed the aircraft in a safe position to land. It is much better to "go around" than risk a landing out of an unstable approach. Go arounds feel like a take-off right before landing because that's exactly what happens, the pilot winds the engines up to near take-off power and the plane flies away from the ground. Simply a landing that becomes a take-off.

**GPS**  Global Positioning System. A constellation of orbiting satellites transmitting extremely accurate positioning information identifying the aircraft location to within mere feet across the globe. Forecast to eventually replace ground based navigation aids.

**GPWS**  Ground Proximity Warning System. The system that utilizes forward-looking radar to warn pilots of upcoming high terrain or the approaching ground. Newer system of EGPWS enhances GPWS with addition of high terrain computer database coupled with satellite position information to give even more advanced terrain information to pilots to prevent inadvertent flight into the ground.

**ground speed**  As a passenger, the important speed; that which measures the speed of the plane across the ground. The higher the ground speed the faster you will arrive at your destination.

**ground stop**  ATC jargon for "stop all planes still on the ground." Used as a means of alleviating congested airspace either now or forecast to occur at a selected destination. May occur as a result of ATC radar failure in the airspace, weather, or too many planes (traffic).

**holding**     A means of temporarily delaying planes en route by having them fly precisely defined racetrack patterns in the sky.

**jet stream**     A river of fast-moving air, often more than 100-200 miles wide, usually between 30,000 and 35,000 feet above the ground. Jet stream winds have been clocked at over 150 miles per hour. They often generate much of the turbulence felt at high altitude, especially along the edges of this fast moving mass of air where eddies, like those along the edge of a stream, make for rapidly changing wind directions and speeds and thus, turbulence. Jet stream winds are most powerful in the winter months and slow down by more than half during summer months.

**knot**     Term for nautical mileage speed measurement. One nautical mile is 6,000 feet vs. 5,280 feet for a statute mile. Originally conceived as a way of measuring a ships speed. Knots were tied on a long rope in measured lengths. As the ship would move through the water, a portion of the rope was thrown into the water and the number of knots pulled overboard by the drag of the water was noted over a given period. This gave the sailors a measure of the speed they were traveling. Now used as the measurement to travel one nautical mile.

**MEL**     Master Equipment List. A list of items prepared by the FAA and the airline that can be out of service and not adversely affect the safety of a flight. Certain equipment may impose restrictions on the time or type of weather the plane can fly in until repairs are made.

**minimums**     Term describing the "minimum" visibility required by the FAA to start and fly an approach. Usually measured in whole miles or fractions of miles as viewed from the ground. More precise approaches require equipment which use light beams to more accurately measure visibility right at the runway and these machines are called transmissiometers. Their measurement is called Runway Visual Range (RVR).

**Minimum Vectoring Altitude (MVA)** The minimum altitude an ATC controller can descend your aircraft to, due to close proximity to high terrain such as mountains, mesas or man-made obstructions such as high buildings or antenna towers.

**originator** A term used to describe a plane, which has overnighted at a location and subsequently leaves on its first flight of the day. (As opposed to a plane, which flies into town, picks up its passengers and then departs.) When a plane starts its workday.

**packs** The air conditioning units, usually located in the lower fuselage, that provide heating and cooling as well as the pressurization to keep the cabin pressure comfortable for the passengers. Powered by compressed air "bled" from a jet engine.

**pitch** The vertical movement of an airplanes nose or tail about the lateral axis (along the plane of the wings). Pitch is controlled by the horizontal stabilizer and the movable part of that stabilizer known as the "elevator." (See Figure 24)

**pitch angle** The angle of the nose of the aircraft up or down as measured from level. The take-off pitch angle would be the difference between the plane on the runway before the nose has left the ground and the angle at which the plane flies off the runway.

**pushback** The task of using a tractor, called a tug, to physically push the plane away from the gate. Some airlines use the jets engines to power the plane back and, amazingly enough, this is known as a powerback.

**radar**
Acronym for RA(dio) D(etecting) A(nd) R(anging), the system used by Air Traffic Control (ATC) to track aircraft. Also used onboard aircraft to identify weather ahead. Senses objects and their movement by sending out a beam of microwave energy (much like those found in a microwave) and sensing reflected energy signals.

**radome**
The fiberglass nose of the aircraft that the radar antenna sits behind. Fiberglass is a "composite" of resin and fiberglass that appears as transparent as glass to radar, thus allowing it to see the weather. Stealth aircraft are built with lots of these composites, which help them hide from radar.

**roger**
Radio response meaning all of last transmission has been received. Not meant to be used as a yes or no response. "Affirmative" or "Negative" is used instead for concise understanding between parties.

**roll**
The left/right (as facing fore or aft) rolling movement of an airplane about its longitudinal (front-to-back) axis, as when it banks for a turn. Roll is controlled by the ailerons and assisted in certain situations by the spoilers acting on the descending wing during a turn. (See Figure 24)

**rudder**
The moveable rear portion of the vertical stabilizer.

**slipstream**
The air or "airflow" blowing by the outside of the airplane.

**spoilers**
Flat, square, metal panels that are mounted on the upper surface of the wing that tilt up to disrupt airflow over the wing. This acts to "spoil" lift and either increase the descent rate of the aircraft or

slow the plane. (Flight spoilers: a portion of the spoiler array on the upper wing surface.) Upon landing the ground spoilers deploy to slow the aircraft and kill virtually all lift upon touchdown, thus placing much of the aircraft weight upon the wheels to maximize braking effectiveness. (Ground spoilers: the entire spoiler array.) Flight spoilers also help the aileron to kill some of the lift on a wing to bank the aircraft by deploying only slightly on one wing alone. You can see them at work inflight, usually in steeper banked turns (usually performed closer to the airport). The lower banked wing may exhibit slightly deployed spoiler panels (See Fig 11, 23).

**squawk**
The four-digit code sent by the aircraft transponder to ATC as a discrete identification code identifying your aircraft, like the license plate on a car. Also used to send ATC discrete predetermined messages in the case of radio failure.

**stability**
The tendency of a vehicle to want to continue in the same direction of travel either in a steady state or when acted upon by another outside force.

**slot time**
See "flow time."

**transponder**
A device which sends a code to ATC identifying your aircraft and indicating what your altitude is. This information is tied with radar position information and shows up on the ATC controllers radar scope identifying your call sign (identification), altitude, speed and direction. In addition to this information is your "squawk code" (see "squawk").

**tug**
A powerful tractor used to pull the aircraft on the ground. Also used to "push" the aircraft away from the gate during engine start.

| | |
|---|---|
| **vector** | Instructions issued by ATC to pilots to turn their aircraft to a specific heading. ATC radar depicts a view of the aircraft traffic from above. Using this "God's eye" view, ATC keeps all the aircraft in an orderly manner and separated from one another. |
| **vortices** | A swirl of wind streaming back from a plane's wingtip very similar to a small tornado. Vortices whip the jet exhaust and the moisture it carries at altitude and aids in making the white contrails so visible from the ground. Vortices trails usually descend behind the plane generating them but can, on occasion bounce off the ground and climb back into the sky. Vortices usually dissipate within a minute of two of the plane's passing while the contrails, if any, may remain for hours. (See figure 7) |
| **wake turbulence** | Turbulence left by an aircraft ahead (like the wake of a boat). Usually in the form of the spinning vortices off the wingtip. May also be jet blast from aircraft that just departed the runway you are landing on. Not a problem affecting control of commercial jet aircraft of like size. The cause of most sudden bumps right after take-off or during landing behind another plane. Also felt at cruise altitude as one good solid bump or occasionally two if both wing vortices are hit. |
| **yaw** | The left-right movement of the nose of the aircraft as when it taxies on the ground. A car spinning on ice "yaws" in rotation. Yaw is controlled by the vertical stabilizer and the movable portion of the stabilizer called the "rudder" (see Figure 23). |
| **zulu time** | Also known as Coordinated Universal Standard Time, a means of keeping the whole world on one clock. Zulu time happens to be whatever time it is in Greenwich, England, the location of the Greenwich Observatory. |

# Acknowledgments

This author would like to express his sincere appreciation to those who have helped make this work possible. An idea may spring from one person's mind, but it is almost always a team effort that makes that dream a reality.

To those dear friends and co-workers who helped with early drafts, thank you so much for your encouragement and time.

Further thanks to Jim Federer, Roger Ways, Mike Campbell, Lewie Webb, Mr. & Mrs. Ray Burns, Mike Ringstorf and all the maintenance technicians (Steve, Steve and Jack) I prodded with questions throughout development of the manuscript. To all the Flight Attendants who read drafts, made suggestions and offered encouragement, thank you all.

Thanks to Stephanie Mudgett and the good folks at Boeing Aircraft for providing me with the best information, and the best commercial jet aircraft made anywhere.

To Bud Buettner, educator and former aircrew member, who gave me many insightful suggestions and valuable critique, thanks for your time and support. Your suggestions were enormously helpful.

To Rich Wright, who as a frequent business flyer and lifelong friend, helped me flesh out the basic direction of the book and encouraged me to complete it, thanks yet again buddy. You're the *best*.

Thanks to the incredibly patient and helpful Ronda Parks for her proof-reading skills. Without her dedication to correct grammar this book would have resembled a mid-fifties Japanese instruction manual. She too was a nervous flyer and provided keen insight into what information might prove useful. I am blessed to have had the chance to meet and work with her.

To my illustrator John Robinson, thanks for the tremendous effort. You turned my fuzzy concept doodlings into polished illustrations. The nine months it took me to find you was well worth the wait. Thanks to you for your dedication to the project and your gift of artistic insight, which made my message to the reader vastly more understandable.

Christy Moeller-Masel deserves all the credit for my cover. She is a true artist and but another one of the neat and incredibly talented people I met while creating this book. Christy introduced me to Lisa Liddy at The Printed Page, who did the wonderful job of converting my Word files into the book you hold in your hand.

Without the mentoring and guidance of Ralph Tanner, a veteran of over 50 years in publishing, I most assuredly would still be standing at the starting gate with no idea how to go about getting a manuscript published. Ralph's tutelage and kind suggestions made this whole hazy concept come to fruition. I will forever be indebted to him for his unfailing support and time donated during final editing. What can one say about another human being but that they gave their most precious asset; their time? This book is many magnitudes better because of his attention.

Most importantly, I would like to thank my wife, Louann, and daughter, Allison who put up with my many hours away from them during the creation of this book. Their steadfast support and belief in my vision was critical. I know there are angels on this earth; I live with two of them. To Gizmo and Maggie (my fur-piggy cats), you were good company during those long early hours at the computer.

Finally, I would like to thank the nervous lady who boarded my deadhead flight to Albuquerque in August of 1999. She was en route to visit her ill father and time dictated that she fly rather than drive. During this flight she professed to me her total fear of flying. After I explained to her many of the topics discussed in this book, she encouraged me to write them down to help nervous flyers like her. Hopefully, I have done my job.

It is the passengers who make my incredible job possible.

Let no one in this industry forget.

Captain Ray Stark

# Disclaimer

The following book is a compilation of the author's own thoughts and ideas. This book should not be construed as any "official" airline material. The author is not a spokesman for any airline and the book you hold in your hand is solely the result of the author's efforts, research, and thoughts. Make no mistake, the views, opinions, suggestions, thoughts, and ideas reflected herein lie solely with and spring solely from, the author, Nothing in this book is in any way connected with any official airline policy, procedure, custom, suggestion, slogan, marketing effort, training program or political viewpoint.

All facts, rules, procedures, and informational data contained herein were believed to be correct at the time of publishing. Things change constantly in this industry and for the latest information or regulation, please don't hesitate to ask the airline you intend to fly on at the time you book your flight. If the reservations agents can't answer your question, they should make every effort to direct you to someone who can.

---

For those interested in aviation as simply a hobby or as a possible career, contact the following organizations for more information:

Aircraft Owner's and Pilots Association (AOPA)
    www.aopa.org

Experimental Aircraft Association (EAA) The Leader in Recreational Aviation
    www.eaa.org
    Young Eagles (Youth introductory flights): 877-806-8902
    Education: 920-426-6570

Women In Aviation, International (WIAI)
    www.waia.org

Be A Pilot: The Introduction to Flying Program for Those Interested in Becoming Pilots
    www.beapilot.com

Virtual Skies, A NASA site great for high school students and others seeking more information on General Aviation
    http://VirtualSkies.arc.nasa.gov

---

## Note to the Reader:

The author is very interested in making *This is Your Captain Speaking* the best possible resource for airline passengers. Please send your thoughts and or suggestions to him at captainstark@earthlink.net.

### *This is Your Captain Speaking*—Special Availability

This book is available for purchase at special quantity discounts in bulk purchases for educational or corporate use, as well as fund raising, resale, promotional, or premium use. Special editions or book excerpts can also be created to fit specific needs.

For details, write:

> Carefree LLC Book Publishers
> P.O. Box 3518
> Carefree, AZ 85377
> or via e-mail at captainstark@earthlink.net

Individual copies may be ordered from thisisyourcaptainspeaking.com. Resellers may order from this site after account authorization.